Children, Divorce
and the
Church

Creative Leadership Series

Children, Divorce and the Church

Douglas E. Adams

Creative Leadership Series
Lyle E. Schaller, Editor

Abingdon Press/Nashville

CHILDREN, DIVORCE & THE CHURCH

Copyright © 1992 by Abingdon Press

This book is printed on recycled, acid-free paper.

Library of Congress Cataloging-in-Publication Data

Adams, Douglas E.
    Children, divorce & the church / Douglas E. Adams.
        p.   cm.—(Creative leadership series)
    ISBN 0-687-06480-5 (pbk.: alk. paper)
    1. Adult children of divorced parents—Pastoral counseling of.
    2. Divorce—Religious aspects—Christianity. I. Title. II. Title:
    Children, divorce, and the church. III. Series.
    BV4463.65.A22   1992
    259'.1—dc20   92-7549
                                                                           CIP

To Linda and Jennifer
Thanks for the love and patience.

Foreword

Four trends have radically changed the parish ministry over the past several decades. The first, which is more apparent to people born before 1930 than to those born after 1940, is that adults of today are far more open to seeking help with their personal, family, and emotional problems than were the adults of the 1940s and 1950s.

A second trend first surfaced in 1946 when 610,000 divorces were granted, compared to only 264,000 in 1940 and 382,000 in 1956. That peak year for divorces was dismissed, however, as a one-time aberration due to the end of World War II in 1945. It was not seen as the signal for a new life-style. In 1969 that record number of divorces set in 1946 was broken with 638,000 divorces, up from 584,000 in 1968. In 1975, for the first time in American history, divorces exceeded a million in one year. In 1981, the current record of 1,213,000 divorces was set, almost double that startling total of 1946.

In 1991 the population of the United States included approximately 53.6 million married couples. That number has been increasing by a net of approximately 350,000 annually for the past few years. That increase is the product of approximately 2,450,000 marriages annually, minus 1,180,000 divorces annually, minus 925,000 marriages that are terminated by the death of one spouse every year.

Since most of the marriages terminated by the death of a

spouse leave no children under eighteen behind, the big issue today is not orphans or half-orphans (the term applied to children with one deceased parent). The number of orphaned children under age eighteen with both parents deceased has dropped from 77,000 as recently as 1960 to 25,000 in 1990. The number with one deceased parent has dropped by a third in three decades from over 3.3 million in 1960 to under 2.2 million in 1990. By contrast, the number of children under eighteen years of age living with a divorced, but not remarried, parent has nearly tripled in only two decades from 4.4 million in 1970 to over 11 million in 1990.

More significant, but less visible, is the fact that in the 1990s, for the first time in American history, the population includes record numbers of adults who as children were the largely ignored victims of traumatic divorces back in the 1970s and early 1980s. Those numbers will be increasing in the years ahead as the children of the divorces of the 1980s grow into adulthood.

The third, and perhaps the most widely discussed, of these four trends has been the emergence of tens of thousands of mutual support or self-help groups. These include support groups for the adult children of an alcoholic parent, for husbands or wives going through a painful divorce experience, for parents who have experienced the death of a child, for employees who have been dismissed by their employer and are now jobless for the first time in their lives, for people who are seeking a new role in life, and many others who are open to talking about their problems.

The big omission from that list is the mutual support group for the adolescent child who is a victim of a traumatic divorce. This book has been written from an insider's perspective to describe that need. It also has been written from the experience-based wisdom, insight, and skills of a pastor who knows how to speak constructively to other pastors and to church leaders so they can respond creatively and helpfully to this still largely ignored need. In simple terms, the author,

Doug Adams, has been there. He knows the subject. He has been a victim. He also has been a pastor to scores of other victims.

The fourth trend is the still small but rapidly growing number of Christian congregations that have accepted the responsibility for the creation, nurture, leadership, and oversight of mutual support groups as an essential, legitimate, and redemptive component of their ministry and outreach. They combine the insights from the helping professions with the redemptive love of God expressed through Jesus Christ as they expand their seven-day-a-week programming through mutual support groups. While this is not the reason for doing it, these churches also have found that the creation and nurture of mutual support groups as an integral component of their ministry has turned out to be an effective means of reaching and serving the generations of people born after 1955.

What is your congregation's ministry with that rapidly increasing number of children and youth who have been the innocent victims of a traumatic divorce? How do these children perceive the church? What can your church offer them? What can your pastor do?

This book is but one in a series designed to help leaders, both volunteer and paid, expand their ministry to a changing world and to people who need to hear the Good News of Jesus Christ.

Lyle E. Schaller

Yokefellow Institute

Contents

Introduction

On the summer afternoon that my mother asked my father to leave our house she also called our pastor. The pastor was a man that I truly looked up to, and in some respects, he set me on my course in ministry. He, like all good ministers, responded to Mother's call within the hour. He greeted our tearful lot with his usual look of wisdom and strength. He asked politely to speak to our mother alone. Nearly an hour and a half later he emerged from our house. He passed quietly by while making his way to the car and drove away. He never once, during the ensuing year, asked my two brothers, my sister, or me how we were dealing with the divorce. He did not know how to deal with children in divorce, and many still do not understand their pain and searching.

The National Center for Health Statistics estimates that nearly 40 percent of American marriages will end in divorce. Of the children in these unions, 67 percent will live in a separated or divorced family before they reach the age of eighteen. Millions of men, women, and children are now living in stepfamily situations. These fixed numbers do not tell the whole story of children and divorce.

As a pastor and a child of divorced parents, I see these numbers in a different light. These figures cannot begin to measure the pain and heartbreak that divorce causes. They cannot begin to measure the lost family structure or a child's rapid move toward sudden maturity. These numbers did little to calm the frantic fears of a young boy who thought his secure, structured world was about to come crashing down around his ears.

The sudden impact of divorce can be overwhelming to children. The shock of realization that all that is familiar is about to change can send some children into a tailspin from which it takes considerable time to recover. The sinking feeling that accompanies the loss of a loved one is the only true description that can be offered.

The motive in writing this book is the hope of sharing a perspective of divorce that is all too often overlooked or ignored. It is difficult to realize that divorce leaves victims other than the ex-spouse. The children of divorce are also victims. They are victims of change where they had no choices; victims where the important players in their lives are torn from the careful scripting of the American idea of family. Pieces of their lives that previously represented the total idea of family are now scattered to the winds of change.

These children are now a part of everyday life and a part of our churches. Their numbers represent a considerable body of recovering victims of divorce. The parents of these children are also suffering the pain of divorce and separation. They are all an integral part of congregational life across the country. Ministry to both the parents and the children of divorce is sorely lacking. There is also a lack of a knowledgeable understanding of their current condition. The wide-reaching effects of divorce on children are just now being considered. In the lives of these children of divorce, what is the role of the parish and its congregation and its pastor?

All too often clergy may be called upon to counsel with an angry wife or a jealous husband. Their time is well spent helping to search for ways to hold a sinking marriage together. But how often do they risk talking to the children? The children are also in need of a listening ear and some wise counsel, before and after the fact. How far a pastor can counsel the parents and the child is limited only by his or her own reading and expertise.

If the pastor from our church or a youth leader had taken the time to talk with me, I may have dealt differently with my parents' divorce. Clergy, parents, and friends are able to make a difference in the lives of these young people. These caregivers may be the ones who are able to help children deal constructively with the divorce and give them some hope for the future.

Though considerable years have passed since my parents' divorce, the scars are still evident today. Change is inevitable, but one learns from the changes. Children are all still the same, but so are the ramifications of divorce. All the same signals and flags emerge with children of divorce. How long the children struggle with the effects of a divorce is still open for speculation. Open to us is the opportunity to help these victims of divorce recover from the harshness of a failed marriage and recapture the rich wonder of living.

Why individuals get divorced is just as much a concern as the children who are affected by the divorce. The reasons can vary from family to family. Some of the chief reasons for divorce may be infidelity, abuse, abandonment, alcoholism, drugs, or stress. But the reasons given for the divorce may not be the real cause of the breakup.

In a recent study by the National Center for Health Statistics and the National Institute on Alcohol and Alcoholism, problem drinking was cited as a cause of many divorces. The study concluded that three times as many separated and divorced individuals were married to a problem drinker. The government survey also stated that 56 percent of the separated or divorced couples had been exposed to alcohol some time during their marriage.

But alcohol cannot be singled out as the greatest contributor to divorce. Some marriages end because of infidelity or irreconcilable differences as well. Yet these may not be the real causes of the divorce. Many of the couples who come to the church office for counseling have grown too far apart in their marriages. Many couples do not know how to communicate with each other to solve their common differences. Individuals turn to alcohol, drugs, and adultery to get away from the real issues that confront them. When these couples cannot face the challenge of recovering their marriage, they choose to separate and divorce. But the divorce may be a more difficult journey than working through the difficulties of the marriage. When children are involved, the stakes become greater and the journey more difficult.

I

Children Don't Get Divorced!

That afternoon when Marie came home from school, she didn't expect to find her mother crying in the living room. She was confused and afraid. Her mother sobbed uncontrollably, and Marie was unable to make any sense of her muffled words. A sinking feeling began to rise in Marie's stomach as all sorts of thoughts raced through her mind. Had her grandmother died, or an uncle? What of her sister, who was not yet home? Her mother continued to sob as she held her daughter. Suddenly the words started to tumble from her mother's lips. "Your father . . . your father is leaving." The secure world as Marie knew it was about to change, as well as that of her parents.

Similar scenes have been played out daily for years. Others have, no doubt, heard some of the same stories repeated in the church study or related by a friend. Divorce does not come neatly packaged. Divorce comes within the folds of everyday living. Divorce comes to the person down the street, to family and friends, and unfortunately to the members of many local churches. In spite of our seemingly calm everyday existence, divorce continues to take its toll on the American family. Marriages continue to fail at an alarming rate. Children of these unions will be the unwitting victims of their parents' divorce.

. . . . . . Enee . . . Menee . . . . Minee .

Children do not get divorced; parents do. Children are the ones who have very little to say in the matter. They are set upon a roller coaster of emotions. The security of their world is suddenly rocked to the very foundation. Fears and anxiety run at a fever pitch as the children try to sort through the clouds of guilt and resentment. It is difficult for children to deal with sudden change. Their security is based on their parents, their home, and their school. Divorce may negate all the consistency on which they had come to expect and depend. The damaging effects of divorce may never be thoroughly understood.

However the divorce may have come about, the effects on the children are still the same. Guilt, resentment, loneliness, rejection, fear, and anger are just a taste of what may come. Add to this the possibility of remarriage by one of the parents, and the whole scheme of things begins to change. By understanding some of the complexities faced by children in divorce, you can begin to appreciate their dilemma.

Do not assume that the difficulties of divorce are limited to the children. Parents suffer similar traumas during the divorce, as does the entire extended family. Divorce is separation and is similar to the grief experience. Parents will be separated from their children. Mothers and fathers will feel the struggle of visitation and the guilt of the divorce. All kinds of new issues are raised during the divorce. Throw a rock into a pond and see how far the ripples reach out. Divorce touches all areas of our lives.

When dealing with the issue of children and divorce, one must see the whole picture, as well as the frame. The causes of divorce are varied, but the effects are similar. With some divorces the effects on children can be healthy and welcomed. In a marriage where the safety of the children is in question, divorce can be understandable and a welcome relief. The children may actually benefit from the divorce. This may give them a chance to have a stable environment. The children may still experience some ill effects from the divorce, but the larger picture reveals more opportunities for a normal life-style.

Even with the extreme rate of divorce in our society, it is possible for parents to achieve a healthy divorce with their children in mind. The essential object of divorce is to separate oneself from the spouse. When parents take the time to think about their decision and what impact the divorce will have on their children, the initial reactions of the children may well be altered. Parents need to think of their children throughout the whole divorce process. If parents think they can put their children on hold and try to start over after the divorce is finished, they are misperceiving troubles. Many of the effects of divorce on children occur early on in the process. A divorce can be healthy when the parents take the children into account from the start.

Many parents may make definite mistakes during the divorce. Some parents assume that the divorce is theirs and that the children do not need to know what is going on.

Parents have the privilege of divorcing, but they should not go along with the assumption that the children should be kept in the dark all along the way. "It is the parents' choice," a mother once said, "and I do not need my children telling me what to do." This is the heart of the issue for children and divorce; they do not have a choice. Many parents are making important moves in their own lives and are not taking the children into account. The problems of mistrust, guilt, and resentment start at this point. All too often the children are expected to endure the trauma of divorce and simply pick up where they had earlier left off. Some parents choose not to communicate on major decisions that affect the children. They may move from the neighborhood, change schools, and lose a parent all in one moment. If possible, children should be made aware of the changes that are about to take place in their lives.

Helping the children to understand the divorce is probably the most difficult concern. Many children will ask questions for which there are no easy answers, but they must be allowed the freedom to ask these questions without fear of reprisal. Children feel much anxiety and fear early in the divorce. All sorts of worries start to enter their minds and hearts. They become scared about their future and sometimes become very angry over the situation. When parents are aware of some of these difficulties, they take time to listen to their children's questions. During this difficult time, no child's questions should be considered stupid. This is a time when the parents can reassure their children that their love for them has not changed. Children need to know that someone is still there, listening to them, building self-esteem, and caring about their feelings.

When parents take time to help their children through the divorce, they may cope a little better. On the other hand, if parents choose not to include their children in the divorce process, they may be encouraging more emotional difficulties. Children will learn from the divorce, both good and bad lessons.

Whether they realize it or not, parents can and will set the tone for their children's understanding of the divorce. How a child will react to the parents depends on what one parent is saying about the other. When a parent constantly down-grades the ex-spouse, the children will pick up on it. They will learn how to hate or mistrust the other parent. Sometimes they will turn completely away from the other parent.

Children learn anger, resentment, and mistrust from the parent who criticizes the ex-spouse. Grandparents who might talk about the ex-in-law in degrading terms may inadvertently add to their grandchildren's confused feelings as well. A loose remark about the other parent paints a picture that is in stark contrast to the one the child may hold.

Divorce has a strange way of bringing the oddness out in people. One aunt once remarked to me that my parents would still be together if I had not been born so soon. Thus I thought that I had been the major cause of my parents' divorce. My guilt was tremendous!

Conversely, children can learn the opposite from a divorce. The parent who takes pains not to "bad-mouth" the other parent is moving in the right direction. Children can learn love, trust, and forgiveness from the way the parents choose to communicate. A parent should talk with the children honestly and try to reinforce their relationship with the other parent. This may be difficult for the parent to do, but the reason for the divorce was not to separate the children from the other parent. The children now have the chance to cope better with the present circumstances, knowing that they can feel all right about their parents.

The balance between divorcing a spouse and helping the children to cope becomes a perilous journey. It is hard to determine who wins, because it is a winless situation. The parent loses a spouse and must start all over. The children lose a parent and sometimes a stable environment. It becomes increasingly more difficult to cope with the pressure. Both the parents and the children feel the pain of change and adjustment to the divorce. Frustration runs high for everyone involved. Tempers are short, and little thought is given to the ultimate outcome of the situation.

During all the trauma and pain of the divorce, the parents, as well as the children, need the stabilizing effects of the congregation. How does the local church relate to divorced families? Are our churches open and caring about these struggling families? I would have appreciated the help and comfort of our own Methodist church at the time of my parents' divorce. As it turned out, the congregation was very divided over who to turn to and help first.

Both my parents were actively involved in the life of our church. My mother sang in the choir, and my father sat on various committees and taught Sunday school. The church was shocked by my parents' sudden divorce. We appeared to be the typical family down the street. There was a great deal of gossip and questioning about the divorce from well-meaning church members. Throughout the divorce process, the church remained vigilant to its own purposes, unable to cope with the divorce.

Years ago, this seemed to be the scenario for the local church everywhere. The church has now come to the point where it copes with the issues of divorce, but it still struggles with the participants. We continue to see divorced families in the church today, but at a much higher rate. We have seen families leave the church over divorce and new stepfamilies taking their places. How can we keep separated families in the life of the church? How does the church minister to families of divorce? What role should the clergy play in helping the children of divorce?

The place of children in divorce is complicated. The issues that arise around them are varied and many, but these children are still a part of the fabric of American life. Their part of this fabric weaves its way through our churches. We see these children week after week, seated in our pews or just hanging around the church house doorway. Maybe they are there because they are still seeking and asking for help. Can we help them and their parents? Are we prepared to listen to their struggle and pain? Can we understand enough of their journey that we can at least point them toward a path that promises hope?

II

Divorce in a Child's Eyes

"Get out! Get out now, and don't ever come back!" Those are the words I remember. I can still hear them ringing in my ears twenty-five years after they split the calm of that summer afternoon. I can see my mother standing at one end of the dining room table, yelling at my father at the opposite end. She turned around suddenly and saw me standing in the hallway. I was not expected there. She had sent us all down to the neighbor's house to deliver Fuller Brush products. She had promised to take us all to the pool when we finished. I finished too soon. She grabbed me by the arm and pulled me outside to the porch. She just sat there crying.

"I'm sorry. I'm sorry," was all she could say. My two brothers came walking down the street with my little sister in tow. They just stood there and stared at my mom sobbing on the porch. After a while I slipped away and back into the house. I heard my father upstairs in the bedroom. I went up the steps and down the hall and stood as still as I could in front of the door. I was scared, and tears rolled down my cheeks. I slowly eased the door open. There was my dad, standing next to the bed, shoving clothes into a suitcase. Where was he going? What was happening here? This had to be a dream. It was not.

That is how my parents started their separation. My father

left the house a few minutes after I had seen him in the bedroom packing his clothes. He did not offer any explanations; he just looked down at me, sitting on the edge of the bed, and told me he loved me. That was the last time he ever told me he loved me.

My mother remained on the front porch until his car rounded the corner and was gone from sight. She looked at us, all teary eyed and dumbfounded, turned around and went back into the house and closed the door. From that day on my life was changed.

Through my eyes, this is how my parents' divorce started. I was only thirteen years old. It happened so quickly that afternoon, but in my mind it all plays out in slow motion. Suddenly you start tumbling through the air, and you do not know if you can stop. There is nothing to hold on to or to reach out for. You feel all alone.

After many years of talking to young people who have been through the divorce of their parents, we know that there are some very visible steps that children go through in divorce. Like the grief process, each step may be a step toward understanding and recovery. These steps do not appear to have a clear sequence or order. You start out with a mass of jumbled emotions and in retrospect begin to sort through them. One cannot place a clear time frame on the process of working through these steps. Fear may be the dominant emotion for a time before loneliness or depression sets in. Some of these emotions run simultaneously in children. Fear, feelings of rejection, hate, and anger may all be evident at one time, with some stronger than others. I know of young people who are still experiencing anxiety over their parents' divorce years after the fact.

We cannot always deal with one set of emotions at a time. Parents are struggling with their feelings at the same time the children are fighting with theirs. Some parents may seem to have had a jump on the situation because they have anticipated or planned for the divorce, but children are often caught completely off-guard. All at once their secure world is shattered by fear and doubt as to what the future will hold for them. We understand why children at first react violently to the news of the divorce. Some children will turn in on themselves and be very difficult to communicate with. Other children will play the martyr and act as if nothing has changed at all.

Age can play an important part in how children deal with the divorce. Younger children seem to adjust to emotional trauma more quickly, if some sense of order is reestablished. Children who are elementary to junior-high age tend to struggle considerably more than their younger brothers and sisters. High school and college-aged persons probably experience the most difficulties with the divorce. They have a larger frame of reference for the family in general. They tend to understand more about their parents, so they experience deeper emotional trauma. I have talked with young people from divorced families who still experience residual effects of a divorce that occurred when they were young children. Some adults can go back and lift out the pictures and the pain of their parents' divorce, years removed from the actual event.

Few children have ever been given the chance to talk about their parents' divorce. They have never had the opportunity to sort through their own emotions and make sense of the current situation. Few parents have realized that they need to take the time to sit down and ask their children what they are feeling. Some young men and women today are still smarting from their parents' divorce, because no one has cared enough to ask them how they feel.

Children have feelings. When a grandparent passes away, the children will be caught up in the emotions of grief and sorrow. Children begin to feel fear and rejection at an early age and will carry these emotions with them as they grow older. Children going through the divorce experience have just as many emotions as the ordinary child. Unfortunately for them, they must also carry some additional emotions, such as rejection, mistrust, and anger, which they may have never had to deal with before. We must begin to see things through their eyes.

Fear and Worry

Among the complexity of emotions that children exhibit during divorce, fear and worry reign supreme. It is hard to imagine a more fearful experience in the life of a child than witnessing the breakdown of the family and home. Fear has been on the list of emotions of every young person who has been through a divorce. Children become scared about what will happen to them and their family. They worry a great deal about the future and what will become of their secure world. When one or the other parent leaves the house to live somewhere else, the children will be frightened about what will become of the parent and whether they will see that parent again. Children will spend sleepless nights worried about themselves or other family members. The fear of change is a constant reminder that something has gone wrong in their family. Some of their fear and worry comes from a loss of control over the situation.

Following the time that my mother asked my father to leave the house, we were all scared and worried about what was going to happen next. My mother was an emotional wreck, which only seemed to complicate our emotions. We could not understand why this was all going on, and our mother did very little to shed light on the situation. We were all left with our own active imaginations and worries.

Guilt

One of the other consistent emotions that children wrestle with during the separation and divorce is guilt. Children center on themselves in their own little world. When that world is disrupted, they often assume the guilt. They seem assured that some action of theirs has had a devastating effect on the family. We all felt guilty. My older brother went out to the curb and brought in the trash cans, which he had forgotten to do for two days. My younger sister and brother started picking up their toys from around the house and putting them away. They must have thought that they could put everything back into order. I went upstairs and started cleaning up my room. We coped with our guilt and grief by staying busy.

Taking blame for the parents' divorce seems to be very common among children of divorce. At some time or another they carry the burden of believing they did something that caused their parents to get divorced. Children are not to blame for their parents' actions during a divorce, and parents must be conscious enough to try to dispel the notion of guilt and blame in their children. Some of the children's fears and worries can be alleviated if the parents reinforce their love for their children and explain the situation clearly. Children are, unfortunately, made to be a focus of blame in some divorces. This is a depressing development. Children are the fruit of a once-happy marriage. How can they so quickly become the objects of blame in the divorce?

Anger and Frustration

Anger and frustration are responses to situations that we do not like or cannot control. Children can become angry during the divorce process; this goes along with the fear and worry that was mentioned earlier. Children will react to the sudden changes in the family. Some children will become quiet and withdrawn, while others will become strong-willed and upset. As the children's fear levels rise, they start to strike out at the people whom they think are responsible for the changes in their world. At times this anger can be difficult for the parents to understand. Why should their children be so angry at them?

Parents need to realize how frightening an experience divorce is to children. A parent may think that he or she is doing the best thing for himself or herself, but it may not be the best thing for the children. People divorce for a variety of reasons. While part of the reason may be for the sake of the children, the child is not usually able to understand this. A child sees only the surface of the situation and how it immediately affects him or her. Being frightened is not the child's fault; these feelings are a result of the dynamics of the situation. These angry children are reacting to drastic changes and threats in their lives.

Children become frustrated because of the changes in their environment. Why does this have to happen? Why can I not see my dad now? If, because of the divorce, the children must leave their home and familiar neighborhood, they will be frustrated and angry. They feel that they have done nothing to deserve the disruption of their world. I know young people who are still angry at their parents for the changes they had to endure. Younger children seem to go with the flow a bit easier. It is the older children who have the most difficult time adjusting to the changes. They question more of the choices that a parent will make. They ask "Why me?" more often. They seem to hold on to their anger much longer than younger children do.

Anger and frustration will be evident in any divorce, but it must be handled. Children, as well as the parents, need a great deal of reassurance during the divorce. Choices are hard for parents to make when they have to make them with the children in mind. Parents must take the time to explain the moves they are making and why. Some children will assume that parents make decisions as a reaction to their child's moods. Some do, but most often change comes out of necessity.

Rejection and Loneliness

At the outset of a divorce most of the attention is focused on the parents and their dilemma. Often, little is said to the children at this point. The quick decisions of who leaves and how soon are left to the parents. For the moment the children are often neglected or forgotten. The principal players, the parents, are caught up in the heat of the battle. The pain, the tears, and the fears of the parents are realized in the initial separation. This is a scary and very traumatic moment for the parents.

The children are in the midst of all of this turmoil. They are frightened and worried. They may be caught up in the hostilities of the situation and become angry and frustrated. Children also begin to feel a certain amount of rejection from their parents. All of the attention is given to the separation and the decisions the parents have made. Now that the process is set in motion, it seems that little can stop it.

As one of the parents packs and leaves the house, the

children's anxiety levels start to rise. "Is Dad leaving because of me?" "Why is Mom crying?" "Will somebody please tell me what is going on?" Serious questions run through the minds of children when the divorce occurs. They are feeling left out of the decision-making process because often the parents don't know what to say to their children. How do we reassure children in the center of all this chaos? It is difficult, but the children must be helped to understand the divorce. The hope is that all parents would be thoughtful enough to help guide their children through this difficult process. However, while some parents do take the time to reassure their children, more often the parents are caught up in their own searching of emotions and find it hard to achieve an even perspective. So where do children turn first? A pastor or a close friend may hear some of those questions from the children. Usually, however, these children turn to themselves as they try to hold the tide of emotions at bay for a little while.

Rejection is a very harmful emotion. Most children are used to a very open and accepting home environment. Rejection does not occur often in the family. Thus children may interpret a parent's leaving as rejection. If they have no way to communicate with the parent, this may reinforce their feelings of rejection. This is especially true if the custodial parent refuses to allow the children to speak to the absent parent. In some cases the absent parent is the one who breaks all communication with the children. Depending on the proximity of the parents, the children may not even see the noncustodial parent for long periods of time. None of these situations will dispel a child's feelings of rejection.

The child who feels rejected may enter a period of loneliness and self-imposed isolation. She or he may withdraw and hope that the present situation will somehow change. If the children have had to relocate to another neighborhood and school system, they may feel even more separation and rejection. The normal course of daily living has changed. When the children cannot deal with the guilt, anger, and frustration, they may very well withdraw and wait it out.

When parents take their children into account, they can minimize some of these feelings. It takes much effort on the part of the parents to think consciously about their children's feelings. When they do this, they can reassure their children that the present circumstances do not reflect on them. The children must be told that they are still cared for and loved, and they remain an important part of the parents' lives. With reassurance comes understanding and listening. The children are now a part of the process and can be made to feel important in the parents' decision-making process.

Loyalty and Resentment

Children in divorce are sometimes placed in difficult positions. Coupled with the emotions of fear, guilt, frustration, and rejection are questions of loyalty and resentment.

When the family breakup occurs, all the clear boundaries of the family are diminished. The father or the mother may leave the household to take up residence somewhere else. In some cases the children are split between the parents, with some of the children leaving with one of the parents.

Perhaps a parent may have visitation rights for weekends only to visit with the children. Perhaps a parent does not accept any visitation and thus chooses not to see the children on a regular basis. There have been some instances where a parent will leave the house and never see the children again.

At this point children begin to question their position in the family and exactly who cares about them. The parent who remains with the children is called upon to perform the dual role of father and mother. The divorce causes some parents to divorce themselves completely from the rest of the family.

This causes some very serious resentment on the part of the children. Add to this the sketchy role of grandparents, and one can see how confused the children must be.

For the first year of my parents' divorce, my brothers, sister, and I stayed with my mother. My father had visitation rights every weekend. On Saturday morning he would come to our house and pick us up. We would spend the day at the movies or the amusement park. My father was living with his parents at the time, so at the end of the day we would go to our grandparents and spend the night. The next afternoon we would return home to our mother.

I hated those visits with a passion. I liked seeing my dad and spending time with him; I hated so much the end of the visit and why it had to end. Every afternoon when we returned home my mom would be waiting at the front door for us. She always wanted Dad to bring us home on time. After we got into the house, the questions would start. Not questions about the time we had with Dad, but questions about our dad and what he was doing and with whom. I dreaded coming home and facing all those questions.

One other thing that bothered me about those visits was the pain it caused my mother. She did not really want us to go with Dad, and we knew it. She would cry every time we left the house on those Saturday mornings. I felt as though I was doing something wrong by visiting my father. We would sneak around to make phone calls to him. I felt disloyal to my mother, but at the same time I felt disloyal for not seeing my father. If I said I wanted to see my father, Mom would be hurt, and if I did not see my father, he would feel hurt. We were caught in the terrible position of having to make choices that children should not have to make. I loved both of my parents and didn't understand why I could not have both of them at home with me.

But not all visitations are bad. Spending time with both the parents is important for the children. This is not a time to dwell on the divorce, but a time to reassure the children that the parents are still present in their lives. If questions are asked by the children, the parents have this time to answer them thoughtfully and with caring.

Divorce hurts children. It is evident that children suffer from divorce in many different ways. Some children will resent their parents for getting a divorce, in the same way that spouses may resent each other for the divorce. Children may resent a father or a mother who chooses not to visit them or call. Children may carry their resentment with them unless parents are willing to help them understand the divorce.

Children should not be forced to make choices between parents. Their loyalty should not be tested. If one parent questions the loyalty of their children, he or she runs the risk of questioning the children's love for both parents.

One afternoon my mother received a phone call from her attorney. He was preparing to finalize the divorce. My mother came into my room and asked me with whom I wanted to live. I said my father, and she left. Less than thirty minutes later she was back in my room dumping my clothes out of the dresser drawers and into a suitcase on the floor. That afternoon I started living with my father at his parents' home. My mother had raised a question that I answered as honestly as I could. She questioned my loyalty, and the results made me question my mother's love for me.

My mother reacted out of her own emotions and never gave me a clear choice. I resented that day for a long time. I understand now why it happened, but it wouldn't have if she had shared her concerns with me. I wish she had taken the time to explain the situation to me. If she had offered to share with me how she had reached this decision, I might have understood better what was happening. As it was, she made her decision alone and never told me why. We should not underestimate the capacity of children to make choices about loyalty.

Several years ago I received a phone call from a young woman who lived in a neighboring community. She had attended a workshop that I conducted a few months earlier. She called that evening with a very odd request. She wanted to know if I would be present at her house when her date came to pick her up for the prom. I was flattered, but was curious as to why she wanted me there. She explained that she had asked her father to be there on this special night. Her mother agreed that this would be acceptable to her. Her dad had refused his daughter's request. Strangely enough, he lived only two blocks away at the time.

The relationship between this young woman and her father is lacking. She resents her parents' divorce because, at the most important times in her life, her father chose not to be a part of her life. Her mother has done all that she can to fulfill her daughter's dreams, but it sometimes is not enough for children of divorce.

Building Hope and Trust

Not long ago I received a phone call from a woman whom I have known for more than ten years. When we first met she was angry and hurting. Then a junior in high school, she was searching her own feelings about her father and the missing pieces of her life. Her father had left her and her mother and sister when she was six years old. Her pain spanned eleven years of struggle. Her father had very little contact with her at that time. She was dating, looking at colleges, and making important decisions about her life. She wanted the influence of a father or at least the security of knowing one was there. She had neither.

Divorce leaves wide gaps in the lives of children. The pieces of father, mother, and family are all there, but somehow the pieces don't fit. All the things one comes to expect about family are altered through divorce. The elements that seem so essential to other families are lost to children of divorce. It may not seem important at the time, but down the road these missing passages can cause pain and harm to these children.

This woman's call reminded me of all the hours and tears that were spent trying to make some shape of her life. She wanted so much to go back and recapture those lost years. She wanted to know what it was like to have a father around the house. She wanted a dad to stand at the front door and size up her date or to hold her when she felt the pain of that first broken heart. The years were so far removed, and the distance from her father seemed too great. In time, though, she found a new strength—one that grew from herself. It gave her new hope and new trust.

Children of divorce do not always bounce back as easily as we may assume. It takes time and listening to help them accept and deal with the situation. As a parent, a pastor, or a friend, you may find yourself listening to the pain and searching of children who have been through their parents' divorce. These children need someone to listen to them and to care. It took months before my friend finally accepted the invitation to come to our home. She was not sure that we were sincere in our caring. She needed to know that she could trust us. She wanted to know that we were serious about our concern for her.

Trust becomes a real issue for children in divorce. They need to know that the people around them are not going to hurt them again. Some want to establish new relationships, but find it difficult to trust their hearts to anyone. Building trust takes time and effort. One must be willing to listen and care about these children of divorce, but with patience and love. All we can offer is hope. The trauma of divorce does not have to affect them forever. In time all wounds heal outwardly. It is the inner pain that must be challenged.

Hope, for children of divorce, is an understanding of what has happened and a mutual search for a way to deal with the pain. The challenge is to help a person see beyond the divorce to know that she or he will survive the tragedy of the divorce. Parents who work with their children through the divorce have a distinct advantage. They have taken the time to explain and to help shape the future. They have left the lines of communication open with their children. The parent who closes out his or her children may be left to pick up the pieces of a broken relationship with the children.

My friend called because she is now thinking of marriage. She has learned to trust and how to have a healthy relationship. She eventually established a relationship with her father. It took work and understanding on her part, and now she is building on the divorce and living in her hope.

Hope is possible if we begin to understand and care about children of divorce. These are fragile hearts, hearts that need the caring of their families and the church.

III.

Helping Children Through Divorce

The fall of David's freshman year at college was filled with excitement and change. He was now on his own at a big university in the east. When David left home, he thought things were going pretty well for himself and his family. Two weeks after mid-term exams, David received a letter from his mother. "Now that you're grown and on your own, we know that you'll understand. Your father and I are getting divorced. We tried to keep everything from you over the years, but it seems that the time has come to stop trying and make some changes in our lives. Love, Mom."

Divorce can occur at any time, on any given day. For David it came as a freshman in college. For Marie it came as a high school student. Divorce has very little respect for age or timing. There is no right time for a divorce. When parents have tried all possible means of keeping their marriage alive, but fail, then divorce happens. Divorce affects younger children at a high rate. With so many divorces occurring very early in a marriage, it is not surprising that most children of divorce are under the age of twelve.

Divorce occurs for numerous reasons. Pastors see and hear about divorce in the church every day. The divorce may involve a member of the congregation or the son or daughter of a member. The parties involved may come to the pastor's

study for counseling or advice, but what will the pastor say? The pastor is a guide, but how are individuals guided down a dark path without some lamp for their feet? If the inevitable is going to happen, how are the children and parents going to be helped through the divorce?

Breaking the News

Even with all the thought and planning that some parents do while choosing to divorce, breaking the news to the spouse and the children is possibly the most difficult task. How does one tell a spouse that love for him or her is gone and that the marriage is ending? To look into the faces of children and say that their mother or father is not going to live with them anymore tears at the heart of any human being. The pain of divorce starts with admitting that the marriage and family are finished. Breaking the news suddenly confirms the difficult decisions that the parents have had to make. After wrestling with every phrase possible, they can find no words that adequately express the decision for divorce.

The news can come in many different forms. Some people leave letters, while others simply leave altogether. Children come home from school to find their mother crying on the sofa or to see the packed bags resting by the doorway. As hard as it may seem, breaking the news to children may be a blessing inside a curse. Breaking the news of the divorce is a necessary evil, but it also begins to set a tone for the future.

No one ever wants to be the bearer of bad news. All too often individuals hear the news of a family member or friend who has died suddenly. The news is a shock. The pain of losing someone through death hurts deeply. How the news is broken can have a significant effect on persons, and likewise how the news of divorce is broken affects how children deal with the divorce.

The responsibility for telling the children that the marriage is over should rest with both parents. When the parents have made the decision to get the divorce, they should both sit down with the children and explain what is going to happen. However, all too often it is left to one parent to break the news of the divorce. It must have been difficult for the mother or father who has had to sit with the children and break the news without the other spouse there. This creates a difficult picture in the child's mind. Where is my father? Why doesn't Mom care about me anymore?

Like David's getting a letter from home, parents have vast choices of ways to break the news. Some parents may have finished the divorce proceedings without ever telling their children. One day they come in and tell their children that they are divorced and that is that. Where are the caring, loving parents then? Divorce will be as much of a shock to the children as it is to the parents. If the divorce cannot be prevented, then it must be shared with the children.

Parents can be constructive if they share the news together. If one of the parents is against the divorce, the children should know. If some parents start out the separation/divorce process by lying to their children and hiding their own pain from the children, they set a dangerous standard. The truth may hurt, but it is the best way to approach this difficult situation. Parents who say that they want to shield their children from the divorce are actually doing more harm than good. No good is accomplished from hiding feelings and mistrusting children's emotions. Most children can handle a divorce if they are told about it honestly.

The parents who sit down with their children and try to explain the situation are trying to be caring and loving parents. The news will be hard to break. The children will ask many questions, and their pain may come out in anger or fear. This is a difficult moment for the parents as well as for the children. This is also a time to reassure the children that they are still loved by both parents. The divorce is not caused by the children, and they must know that. They must know that they are still an important part of their parents' lives. It should be explained to the children that there will be changes and decisions, but that they are a part of those decisions.

David's parents took the easy way out when they wrote to their son at college. In reality they created more problems in the way they handled the news. What David's parents got was a frightened freshman who called home to find out what was really going on. He had to get some of the news over the phone from his mother and then call his father to get the rest of the sad details. David was torn between leaving for home immediately or finishing the semester in pain and confusion.

Why had David's parents not waited to tell him later? What did they think he would do with this information at school? David was angry with his parents for their separating and the way they announced it to him. The semester break was only a few weeks away, and they could have told him then. As it was, he came home later that week to see his parents. By then the air was filled with misunderstandings and resentment.

Laura's parents took some measure of responsibility when

their two daughters learned of their divorce. Laura remembers that her father decided to take Laura and her sister to a favorite spot that the family had shared over the years. Laura's father calmly explained that he and their mom had some problems and that it might be better if he left home for a while. Laura recalls how scared she was at the thought of her father's not being at home anymore.

She was angry and confused all the way home. Both she and her sister sat in the back seat of the car, engulfed in tears. When they reached the house, their mother was waiting for them at the front door. Their father's bags were already packed and resting on the sidewalk. The exchange was dramatic as their dad put his bags in the trunk of the car while the two little girls ran to their mother's arms. A few moments later, their dad's car pulled away from the curb as the girls embraced their sobbing mother on the porch. A little, six-year-old girl and her sister saw their father at home for the last time that day.

Nothing can ever erase the tremendous pain children feel when their parents get divorced. Moments like Laura's will always be etched into their minds and hearts. Had Laura's parents told them about the divorce together, the pain may not have reached as far as it did for Laura. Her memories of that day are just as real today as they were that day. She hated her father for leaving them that day. She was scared and confused when her dad's car pulled away and he never said good-bye. She sat and listened to her mother try to explain what was going on and what would happen to them. The three of them cried the better part of the day, but the next day they started over, together.

When Michael and Stephanie heard the news of their parents' separation, they were both shocked. They sat on the couch in the family room and stared back at their parents in disbelief of what they were hearing. Their mother was crying as their father struggled to find the right words to speak. They had both tried hard to keep the marriage alive over the past few years. They had talked and fought often during the preceding months, but to no avail. The reasons were varied, but the bottom line had been reached.

Finally their mother conceded that both parents were to blame for the failure of their marriage. It was nobody's fault but their own, and Michael and Stephanie were not a part of the problem. Both parents went to great lengths to explain the growing litany of problems and differences between the two of them. They both believed that this was the answer for their present circumstances.

The next hour was filled with tears and confusion for Stephanie and Michael. Their parents tried their best to express their feelings for their children. Michael and Stephanie knew that their parents loved them a great deal. Both parents reassured them that their love would not change, even when one of them left the next day. The parents understood the shouting and tears from their children and tried their best to see past the quick outburst of anger from the children.

Both Stephanie and Michael had gone to their rooms to think and cry, and later that evening they talked again, as a family. The break had given the parents time to reflect on their decision and how they would handle the days ahead. Now that everyone was a little calmer, the questions from the children came easier. What happens next? Where is Dad going to live? Are we going to stay here or move away? One by one each question was answered and promises made carefully. Dad would be close by in an apartment. The rest of the family would remain in the house and continue in the same schools as before. The children could see and speak to their father any time they wished.

Rest did not come easy that night. More questions would come the next day, along with more confusion. But later, Michael and Stephanie would know where they stood in the divorce process. They knew that their parents would still love them and were not divorcing because of them. Changes would be coming soon, but they both believed that their love for their parents would still be the same.

Healthy divorces start with breaking the news to the children. There is no way of getting around the pain that divorce brings, but there are ways of dealing with the pain and turning it toward healing. If a parent starts divorce proceedings without consideration for the children, he or she runs the risk of finishing the divorce without the children. Mistrust, guilt, anger, and resentment can start from the very beginning of the divorce. The effects of many of the fears can be minimized if discussions start with the plain truth, instead of hiding the pain and the reality of the situation.

Explain, Don't Confess

When parents take the time necessary to break the news to their children, they must be prepared for questions from the children. Honesty is still an important ingredient when talking to the children, but honesty does have some limits.

Children need to know the reasons for the divorce, but not necessarily all the causes. They need a clear framework for why the divorce is taking place. The simple explanation that "Dad and I don't love each other anymore" is not enough. Children may realize more than we think. They may have heard the arguments late at night. Some well-meaning relative may have let something slip. It is hard to hide the tension around the house when these things are going on. The causes for the divorce may run very deep for the parents, but the basic reason for the divorce must be the center of focus.

I still do not know why my parents got divorced. My mother always said that she fell out of love with my father. My father could never explain it at all. Why do people get divorced? My parents seemed all right the day before all hell broke lose. Suddenly this ugly monster called divorce knocked at our door and that was that. I wanted to know more. Why did it happen to our family? Why was everything okay one day and terrible the next? As a child I constantly wondered what really had happened to my parents' marriage. I started to mistrust them because they could not or would not tell us what was going on.

The reasons for divorce may be hard to explain, but the parents must attempt to give reasons. There's no need to go into all the details of the break-up, but a plausible explanation will help the children to understand that this was not a hasty decision. Parents must be sensitive about how much information the children can handle. Age is a factor as well as maturity. Older children can understand the dynamics of relationships, while younger children only feel the fear of separation. If particular details are necessary, they need to be explained clearly. Parents should not be surprised if children try to shut the whole thing out and refuse to listen. This will be hard on them, and it may take some time to set the stage.

The goal here is not only to help the children to understand the divorce, but also to help them through the divorce. The more the children can grasp about the divorce the clearer the situation will seem. If the children are left to wonder why and to question the reason for the divorce, they will soon become angry and distrustful of their parents. Explanations are needed to minimize some of the confusion surrounding the divorce. The parents have some clear objectives in getting a divorce. Loss of love is certainly one, as well as neglect, abuse, infidelity, or abandonment. These may be plausible reasons for anyone's divorce, but do the children understand that? It is possible that some do, but children need to be helped through the divorce, not just carried along with the tide.

Reassuring Love

All too often, some parents miss the fact that the children are shaken by the divorce and need to be assured of the parents love and concern. The parents are struggling with their own emotions and are trying to sort out their next move. Questions are being asked where answers simply do not exist. As the fear and frustration levels begin to rise, parents forget to take time to hold their children and let them know that they are still loved and needed. Too often parents start to withdraw from the pain of the divorce and leave their children on the outside. The parents build protective barriers around themselves and try to heal their own wounded hearts. Parents love their children each day, but somehow when a divorce occurs they neglect to reassure them that they are loved. Their children are doing the same thing. They seek a place of refuge where they can deal with their fears. A set of open arms would be a welcome sight at this point.

The role of pastoring comes in clearly here. Pastors are there to reassure individuals of the love of God and Christ the Son. Are not we all called to share this same love with those who are suffering the pain of divorce? If it is known that a divorce is occurring in one of the church families, can the congregation hold them ever so close and try to nurture them through this terrible experience? Pastors know how to help the parents, but they may not be sure of how to help the children.

Congregations can be a very special comfort to divorcing families. In the past these families were not thought of as hurting individuals by the church. In some churches divorced individuals were not made welcome. Today the church is trying to look at these persons differently. Divorced couples and their children need the benefit of a loving, open congregation. Instead of ignoring them, the church is now willing to help these families through their difficulties. Support groups for divorced and single parents are being fostered in many local congregations. Youth pastors and church school teachers are more in touch with children of divorce.

The fear that children experience is that of rejection and loneliness. They see the divorce as a means of removing love and replacing it with pain and confusion. Children need the assurance that their world is not going to be fragmented through the divorce. When one parent leaves the house, the children feel that a part of their loving is gone. Each parent needs to reassure the children that they are still going to be loved by both the custodial parent and the one who is gone.

A pastor, youth leader, or caregiver can help children to sort through their feelings about the divorce. The fears and anxieties children feel through the divorce are real and natural. These children need help to understand their feelings, and they need to be given constructive ways of expressing their fears and dealing with them. A pastor may know the situation better than the children do. A pastor's insight might help the children to understand the divorce and lead them to healthy feelings about their parents. Assuring the children that they are loved will help them through the divorce and the reestablishment of a new home and future. If the children are loved and helped through the divorce, they can deal better with the pain and the confusion.

Making Room for the Other Parent

Someone always leaves the home. One of the parents is missing. In some instances the children are made to leave the home with the departing parent. The separation/divorce process presents a clear division within the family. The children are immediately presented with the difficult decision of loyalty between the parents.

Being home with one parent is reassuring, but what becomes of the mother or father who has had to leave? The children are at a loss as to what to do. The parent who remains with the children may be either a villain or a saint. "Did my mother make my dad leave?" "Dad has stayed with us, while Mom ran off." The children begin to see the parents in a different light. The one who cares stayed, while the one who left was a villain, or vice versa.

When my mother told my father to leave the house, she became the villain. I did not want my father to leave. She became the bad person for hurting my dad and us kids. We treated her like a villain too. In our minds she had the control.

47

She could ask our dad to come back to the house, and everything would be fine, but she did not ask him back.

She disliked the visits we had with our father. I do not think she resented our seeing Dad as much as she hated seeing him come to the house to pick us up. She always wanted to know what we did and where we went. She especially wanted to know everything our father said about the divorce and her. She seemed to turn so hard against our father. This was totally foreign to us. She talked so harshly about our father that it became very painful to love either one of them. If all that she said was true, then why did I think he was so great as a dad?

Parents must remember to make room for the other parent. Children simply are not prepared to hear one parent running down the other. Parents who refuse to allow their children to visit with the other parent are causing serious damage to their own relationship with the children. They should not be expected to react to the divorce situation the same way the parent does. Children are not the cause of the divorce, nor are they weapons in the divorce.

Chad was a sophomore in a Midwestern college. Once a month his mother would call and complain about his father, who was late with the alimony payments or the child support. "Would you please call your father and tell him to pay up?" she asked. Chad would call his father and explain the situation and try to please his mother. His father would always respond, "If your mother wants her money, you tell her to call me." Chad was always in the middle of his parents' divorce. Surprisingly, Chad's parents had been divorced for twelve years. He had to deal with a divorce that was not his, and his parents were not caring enough to see the pain they were causing their son.

Room must be made for the other parent to see the children. This must be done in a healthy environment, free from outside pressures. The choice for the divorce belongs to the parents, but the children must deal with the difficult reality of juggling their parents. They feel a divided loyalty for their parents, and they do not need to. The parent who pushes too hard against the other runs the risk of alienating his or her children in the process. Parents must never use their children to achieve their own goals in the divorce. Many children can see through this and realize that they are just being used. One day they were just normal kids, and the next they were legal pawns in their parents' divorce. More than one child has desired to simply divorce his parents and go it on her or his own.

Divorce is also difficult for the parents. The pain is often tremendous. Some parents make choices that seem realistic and clear to them, but that may not be healthy for their children. It takes some caring and sensitivity to see that the children have a healthy respect for both parents. Parents should try putting themselves in their children's minds and hearts for a while. The parent may feel the uncertainty and confusion that is going on in the children's lives. If one parent makes room for the other, she or he allows the children to sort through the divorce with both of the parents at the same time. Too often, children are left to pick up the pieces of a broken relationship with a father or mother. Either they were denied the opportunity to visit the other parent, or they heard so many terrible things about that parent that they could not decide how to feel about him or her.

If the children are given the opportunity for visitation, they should be encouraged to take it. If they seem worried about visiting the other parent, the custodial parent should find out why. If they are concerned about loyalty or apprehensive about what to do, take some time to help them work through their fears. One thing must be very clear: When parents have the opportunity for visitation, they must also take it. Too many parents neglect the chance to see their children and take part in their activities. Parents do a great deal of harm when they shut their children out and refuse to see them or remember the special moments in their lives. They must care enough to accommodate each other for the sake of their children. It may be hard to be in the same room with an ex-spouse, but it must be done for the sake of the children.

A few years ago, I walked a young woman down the aisle of our church on her wedding day. Her father had broken all contact with her over the years. He had refused time and again to see her and care about his daughter. Now, on the most important day of her life, her father remained at home, unwilling to care. He had burned too many bridges behind himself. Now the moment was lost, but not the memory, nor the pain.

I have graduated once from high school, twice from college, and once from seminary. My parents never attended those graduations. Each was always afraid that the other one would be there, so they decided not to attend. I wanted more than anything for them to be there and be proud of the only child in our family to graduate from college. Not so. I remember those occasions and the pain of missing my parents at the times that I wanted and needed them the most.

Parents can help their children through the divorce if they care to. If they want to take the time to break the news together and start the process with reassuring love and concern, they can help their children. If they want to keep their children after the divorce, parents can care about them while they are going through it. It will not be easy. Some parents' pride will take a beating for the sake of their children. The children will be confused and fearful for as long as we allow them to be.

With caring and honest love, we can help the children of divorcing parents. As parents, clergy, and just simply friends, we can guide them through a difficult experience. It takes time, but that time is well worth the effort.

IV

Mistakes Parents Can Make

Catherine, the mother of two young children, had just suffered through a difficult divorce. She sat in her minister's study, nervously trying to explain her situation. She had just moved to the community and had taken a position as a secretary in a local law firm. She had made the move to get as far away from her ex-husband as possible. All she wanted was to separate herself from the painful memories of the divorce. She had made all her moves and decisions based on her own feelings, never once considering how those changes might affect her children.

Now, all the changes and quick solutions were catching up with Catherine and her children. Her two youngsters were now angry and confused. They didn't want the move or the separation from their father. New schools, new friends, and old pains filled their days. All the changes and questions were now creating resentment and anger at home. Catherine now found herself desperately trying to make sense of her children's anger and pain.

Few individuals have gone through life without making mistakes. Mistakes are made every day of our lives. If someone was there every step of the way to warn us, we might never make another mistake; but there is not always someone there to guide us past the dangers of life. Few

parents can see the pitfalls of divorce or their effects on the children. No divorce has ever been the same as another, but there are some common mistakes that parents may make during the divorce. These common mistakes can affect the way children come to deal with the divorce and how they recover from it.

Clergy, teachers, and youth leaders have the opportunity to help guide individuals past the pitfalls of everyday living. Their guides may be Scripture, wisdom, and experience from living. While dealing with peoples' lives on a daily basis, they have a background for the difficulties that lie ahead for individuals who have made poor choices. Parents do not have that advantage when it comes to divorce. Decision making in the midst of all their emotions is difficult to do. There are self-help books on the market today to tell people how to get divorced. But our role becomes one of helping individuals see past the present situation to how their current decisions will affect their lives as well as the lives of their children.

Most decisions are made in the heat of emotion without time for reflection. Most of the parents I have talked to wish they could have changed some tough decisions made during their divorce. Most wish they had taken more time to think through their decisions. Some wish that they had gotten more advice and direction from an experienced counselor. They understand that the decisions they made had a deep impact on their children and the direction their relationship took. Some of their decisions led to serious mistakes for their lives and their children's lives. It is difficult to go back and change some of those decisions. Words that are spoken in the heat of emotion always seem to linger in the minds of people. The anger and confusion can lead to quick decisions. These hasty mistakes can cause lasting harm to the lives of the children.

Changing Life-styles

Sudden change is usually the first product of divorce. From the time that the first announcement is made, changes start to take place. In most cases a parent leaves. For some the change can involve the children's leaving the home. If parents are aware of their children's feelings, they will measure these moves carefully. Essentially one parent is the first to leave the house, usually in anger. If parents have made an effort to break the news to their children, this move will not be a total shock. Children will still react emotionally to this change. No child ever wants to lose a parent. This is a very difficult experience for children. They know Dad or Mom is still around, but not where he or she should be, in the child's view. Children have a great deal of fear and worry because of this fact. Even when the change has been talked about beforehand, the transition is difficult. So the parents need to be very reassuring at this time.

The parent who leaves must commit to keeping in contact with the children. They must be reminded often that both parents still love them. Children may become very insecure and react with anger and frustration over the changes. Parents need to understand that this is a normal reaction. However, the parents should worry about children who become withdrawn and closed. Children tend to keep a great deal to themselves during periods of change. It is hard to remember that the children are not seeing the divorce in the same way the parents do. It may seem necessary for the parents to divorce, but children cannot see the reasoning. They know that their world is changing rapidly. The home they know is different and that one of their parents is missing. Therefore, they become very unsure about the future. Most parents are unsure of what the future holds as well. They worry about what will happen next and how to handle it. They should not be afraid to share with their children their own feelings about these sudden changes. The children will be more open to sharing their feelings if they see that their parents are doing so as well.

The pastor who might be involved in counseling a divorcing couple needs to guide them in understanding how changes will affect their children. Each move should be measured against how it will affect the children, not how it will benefit the parents. Thought and discussion should be given to the children and their welfare. The pastor needs to continually ask how the children are adjusting to the changes. Sometimes the parents need to be reminded that the children are an important consideration in the divorce. Keep the parents thinking about the children and not just about themselves.

Keep in mind that change can come in several different forms. Though many changes occur when one parent leaves, still more important changes are to come. The security of the home is very important to children. This is their world, and any disruption of it has an effect on them. With the leaving of one parent come changes in the household itself. Suddenly a mother or a father is a single parent. This calls for dual roles. Divorced parents face a challenge that is not very different from dealing with the death of a spouse. There is still pain and grief over the failed marriage. Parents must still deal with the grief of the children and their own insecurities. Parents must not be afraid to be honest about their own pain and suffering. The children will understand some of the emotions the parent is feeling. To try and hide this pain is not beneficial to the parent or the children. The changes have come and must be dealt with in a constructive manner.

In most households, any change that will affect the family is shared with them. Selling the house and moving across town is difficult for most families. Having to attend a new school, living in a new neighborhood, and making new friends may be traumatic for children. The parent who makes sudden changes is missing the opportunity to help his or her children through the divorce. If changes come quickly, with little discussion or warning, the children are caught offguard. A child's finding the car packed when she or he comes home from school is such a sudden move. Announcing a remarriage without any discussion is a devastating change. The children will become defensive and distrustful toward their parents. Often these children will carry deep resentment toward their parents because of the disruptions in their lives. If it is necessary to make a change, the children should be made aware of it beforehand. They may still not like the changes, but at least they will have had the opportunity to vent their frustration and fears. Anticipation of an unwanted change is better than the terror of the unknown. Children need to know enough about changes to help them understand the divorce. Keeping them in the dark may very well keep them from a parent's love later on.

Pastors who are confronted with a divorce in their

congregation know there will be change. In counseling the parents and children involved, the pastor will try to share advice and give comfort. The best advice, at this point, is to take things slowly. Encourage the parents to make decisions keeping in mind the children and how the divorce will affect them. The pastor needs to share with the children the fact that change is sometimes difficult, but give them the hope that you will try to help them understand these changes.

Promises to Keep

In the midst of all this change parents often promise their children guarantees of a better life. Change is not always a guarantee of better things to come. Thus parents should be careful about making promises they might not be able to keep. There is too much unknown about the future for one to make grand promises about what will be.

Few parents can promise their children a wonderful new home, gifts, and the ability to take away all the hurt. It is natural to soothe children's feelings, but promises may become the ultimate hope for children. Promises that are made at the height of emotion are really wishful thinking by the parents, and many such promises are for things the children do not need. Therefore, a parent should not promise anything that cannot be delivered. The noncustodial father who promises to keep in touch with his children every week is making a commitment to his children. It is an important promise, because the children need to hear from their father on a regular basis. Broken promises, like forgotten phone calls and birthdays, or missed visitations or those canceled at the last minute will harm the relationship between the father and his children.

If parents are serious about helping their children through the divorce, they must be more conscious about the hopes they give their children. My mother promised us that we could call our father any time we wished. Every time we wanted to phone our dad, however, she would start to cry and complain that we loved him more than her. Promises should not be used against children. I think my mother was sincere about her promise, but really did not want us to call our father. It hurt her to let us contact him, but it was a promise that we needed to have. When her crying did not stop, we stopped calling.

Too many promises are made as a reward or a bribe. Many parents in nondivorced homes will use some kind of promise as a way to motivate their children to do their chores or homework, but it works differently with children of divorce. A divorced parent should never promise his or her child anything as a reward if it might harm the other parent. Making promises to get information after a parental visitation is a mistake, and using children to get back at an ex-spouse is wrong. In some divorces, the children are made out to be pawns. Promises then become weapons rather than rewards from a loving parent.

Positive Promises

Promises that are made should be positive in nature and borne with considerable thought. It takes some time for a parent to calmly think through what he or she is going to say to the children. If parents would take the time to think through their promises, they might find some positive ones to share with their children.

Love, understanding, and honesty are examples of positive promises. Parents are still parents and must be very careful to reassure their children that their love is a promise as well as a guarantee. Parents would do well by promising to keep the door of understanding open at all times. Children in divorce are confused enough about the situation going on around them; why would a parent not want to help them understand the divorce?

Most parents want the best for their children. A parent's

best giving is done in honesty and truth. Parents cannot guarantee a brilliant future for their children. They cannot always promise to take away the pain of the divorce. They can promise to be there and listen to their children's fears and worries. They can promise to keep the lines of communication open with the absent parent and provide ways of sharing the changes going on in their lives.

Positive promises that are kept will make for a stronger bond between the parent and the children. The parents who break all the promises they make erode the trust the children have in them. It may harm their relationship well into the future. Being positive, clear, and honest is a better promise to keep.

No Chances at Choices

The day my mother packed my clothes and took me to my grandparents' home resulted from a parental choice. At the time, I thought she was choosing for me not to be a part of her life. I thought she didn't want me as her child anymore. Years later I learned that she and my father had worked this all out beforehand. The choice was theirs, but it made me live with my father and not my mother. It never occurred to her or my father that they should discuss this choice with me. No, they decided and that was that.

If parents are in the habit of making promises, they should promise to talk with their children about choices. Choices are the decisions parents make during the divorce that will affect themselves and their children. Choices are good, so long as they are made with sufficient information and a clear head. Choices made in haste and with little concern for the children are poor choices. They will lead to more difficulty down the road.

Most parents make choices based on their own sets of concerns. We all understand these choices and the needs that motivate them, but do the children have a choice? Do the children have an opportunity to share in all the decision making that's going on? It may not seem important at the time, but it will later on. The changes that are going on are important and will set the parents and children on a new course in life. Change brings about choices that are necessary, but it is also necessary to share these with the children.

One of the worst things for a child is to come home to massive change and confusion. The divorce has brought about a devastating choice that the children had little to say about, but it still affects them. I know that many parents believe that they are making choices that they think are good for themselves and their children. What parent would go to a child and ask whether or not the parents should divorce? But after the trauma of the divorce has started, the choices may be more difficult to make and more far-reaching than parents realize. The choices that parents make will have a lasting impact on the children, for good or for bad.

A great deal of thought must be given to the choices the divorcing parents are about to make. Whether the choices involve moving, staying, schools, neighborhoods, or a new spouse, the children need to be involved in the choices. If parents decide to make choices without the children's involvement, they have already chosen to limit their honesty and communication with the children. They have set up barriers to trust and have chosen not to deal with the fears and anxieties of their children. This is a crucial mistake on the part of the parents. At a point when the children are seeking some security in a whirlwind of confusion, their parents are shutting them out of the picture. The children need to be involved, if only as a token gesture. Depending on the age of the children, the choices may or may not have a great impact, but the children still need to be involved in making the choices. The parent needs to carefully spell out the situation and ask the children how they feel. They will gain a better sense that they belong to the family, however fragmented it might be.

Again, parents need to give thought and discussion to the choices they make. If the children are better informed during the divorce, they will be better equipped to make choices of their own in the present as well as later in life. Parents need to realize that rash decisions are just another trauma with which the children must deal. They add to the confusion and pain of the divorce by acting too quickly and without regard for their children. Choices should be explained and understood before they are initiated. The parent who takes the time necessary to explain change is taking time to build a better relationship with her or his children also.

Children in the Middle

David was a confused thirteen-year-old on the day he went to court with his father. He had never been in a courtroom before, but that day was different. He was asked to share with the referee the reasons why he wanted to live with his father and not his mother. He sat, bored, on the hallway bench, trying to remember everything his father had told him the night before. David did not want to do this at all, but he disliked his mother for leaving his father.

Children are a wonderful gift to any marriage. They can bring joy and satisfaction to their parents. If this is true, then why do some parents choose to use their children against each other during the divorce? The lovely children of their marriage now have become instruments of defense and pain. Child-support payments, visitation rights, and alimony are the battlegrounds of divorce, and children are caught in the middle. The angry mother threatens to withhold visitation if the father does not pay alimony. Children are asked to testify in court proceedings against their father or mother. The pain of being a child caught in the middle of a divorce is terrible. Why should these children be made to endure such pain and trauma? These are children, not public property. They are the product of a once-loving relationship and now are the focal point of legal maneuvering.

The real trauma of divorce comes down to the incredible pain of separation from one of the parents. The choices are clear to the parents, but not to the children. In most states, a twelve-year-old child can choose which parent he or she wants to live with, but no one wants to make that choice. These children may question why they should have to choose between one parent or another, but the reality of the situation dictates that such choices must be made.

If couples did not get divorced, there would be no need to wrestle with this issue. But we do have to wrestle with the issues of children in divorce. If the tide of divorce cannot be stemmed, what is to be done? Pastors and teachers see the pain of failed marriages almost daily. Yet all their encouragement and advice on how to work out difficulties in relationships seem to fall on deaf ears. How can clergy and caregivers make parents realize the pain their children might suffer from the divorce?

With the continuing high divorce rate, the number of children involved in divorce grows. Parents are still putting their children in the middle of divorces. They blame them, bribe them, and deny them the necessities of a family life, and it hurts. Families are divided down the middle every day in our court systems. Brothers don't grow up with brothers, and sisters go with their mothers. And the grandparents not only suffer the pain of their own child's divorce, but also may never see their grandchildren again.

As long as there is divorce, children will be in the middle. Parents must be conscious enough to not use their children during the divorce. Children are not pawns to be maneuvered in the courtroom, nor are they weapons with which to bash the ex-spouse. These young lives are suffering the pain of separation just as much as the parents suffer. They are

61

fearful and confused about the divorce. What future they envision will be seen through the tears of the divorce.

If parents choose, they can limit their mistakes. One way to avoid mistakes, as said above, is to take the time to explain decisions to the children, helping them to understand the changes that are taking place and remembering that they are still children. Divorce is not easy for parents or children, but it can be made less traumatic if parents care for their children.

This can also be a building time in the relationship between the parents and the children. The hurt and confusion of the divorce can be taken apart piece by piece. Parents can correct serious mistakes and recover their children's respect and love. Parents can be very reassuring to the children by sharing that they have the same fears and worries. This type of honest evaluation of the situation can bring about much-needed healing. This shared time can give the children an understanding of forgiveness. It can also go a long way in comforting the troubled and insecure hearts of both the parents and the children.

Clergy and caregivers should encourage this type of honest interaction following a divorce. The children may be hurting, but they are not sure how to share that with their parents. They may be angry over a parent's leaving home with no apparent explanation. Sorting through these feelings will help in their recovery from the divorce and set them on a clearer path in the future.

V.

Lingering Side Effects

At the tender age of sixteen, Laura was a bitter young woman. Filled with resentment, fearful of relationships, and very closed, she struggled through life with the pain of her parents' divorce. Laura grew up outside of the typical home. She had dreamed of the days gone by, when a father would be present and share in a family life. Her dreams never came true, so she turned in on herself and wrestled with her own fears and disappointments.

Now she was angry with life and with herself. She wanted to trust people around her, but found it hard to risk herself. She deeply resented her father for all that he had taken from her. She resented his moving so far away from her and never watching her grow up. She was angry with her father for all the pain he had caused her mother and sister, but desperately wanted a relationship with him. She was confused and hurting. Why had all these things happened to her? When would she ever be happy again?

Laura learned a lot from her parents' divorce, and she is still learning. The long-lasting effects of divorce on children are still being reviewed, but the truth is that divorce can have a lasting impact on the lives of children. Millions of children are living their lives today with the residual effects of their parents' divorce. These children are developing relation-

ships based on the information from their experience of divorce. Some people find it hard to develop a healthy relationship because they lack trust in others. Still, they are carrying unresolved pain from their parents' divorce. They will take the pain out on the world around them or on themselves. They become closed and afraid to risk their own hearts to anyone at all.

Children of divorced parents learn from the experiences around them. Parents who are not helping their children through the divorce are adding to the pain and confusion of their children. Children will see and hear a great deal of anger during the divorce. They will feel some emotions for the first time and not know what to do with them. They will learn some of the wrong lessons from the divorce situation unless a parent, friend, or pastor is there to help them along the way. Parents should be encouraged to seek help for their children, if not from the pastor, then from the school psychologist or a local divorce support group. It is difficult for parents to deal constructively with their own emotions and still see that their children are working through the divorce. If the parents cannot help their children through the divorce, it may fall to a youth leader or teacher to make sure that some guidance is made available to them.

These lessons from divorce will influence the future decisions and attitudes of many. Some children will carry the pain of the divorce into their own adult relationships and marriages. By being aware of some of the hidden traumas children of divorce carry with them, we might be able to clear a straighter path toward the future and help to ease their pain. Again, our role as pastor, parent, or friend is to listen with a caring ear. Parents may hear things from their children, years after the divorce, that they did not even know had affected them. Pastors hear the pain of people's lives every day, and thus know that unresolved conflict that is never healed can damage individuals forever. If we listen, we will understand that the pain of divorce can go on for years.

Resentment and Anger

Resentment and anger are emotions that consume many children of divorce. Like Laura, some children keep their anger and resentment inside themselves for a long time. The pain of a broken home is not easily forgotten. The fears and confusions are compounded by the parents' separation. When a parent does not talk through the divorce and reinforce the importance of the other parent, the children will imagine their own explanations. Some children, years later, feel that a parent left the home because of them and not because of the divorce. They are angry at themselves and feel guilty about the divorce. Children will resent a parent who leaves and then has very little contact with them. Children will become angry and distrustful of a parent who makes nice promises and then does not deliver.

Laura's resentment and anger were natural, predictable,

and normal. They grew from having a father who left the house and never came back. Laura's father made all kinds of promises of a new life and then did not deliver. He took very little interest in her life or her development as a young woman. It was a struggle to get him to come to her high school graduation. To compound her pain, her father remarried a woman who resented the presence of a daughter from a previous marriage. Laura feels forgotten and betrayed by her father, and she stayed angry at him for years. Not until someone was willing to take the time to listen to her did she start to resolve some of the pain and resentment she felt.

Children should be allowed to talk about their anger and resentment. Someone needs to listen to them. Whether it is in a divorce support group meeting or while sharing an ice-cream sundae after school with the pastor, these children need to find someone to listen to them. When parents listen to their children, they can help them to understand their feelings and keep them from getting misdirected. When children can see their anger and resentment and deal with these emotions early on, their future may be brighter.

Mistrust in Relationships

Trust is important in any relationship. Children of divorce value trust above all other emotions. For them, trust is a very fragile commodity. They have based their lives on trusting their parents and the firm foundation of the home. When divorce occurs, their trust level is shaken. Too many changes are taking place in their lives, and too many decisions are being made for them. When a parent leaves the home, the child's trust level is nearly destroyed. The child turns toward the remaining parent for reassurance that his or her trust is well placed. If that parent abuses that trust, the child may never learn to trust anyone again; his or her fate seems sealed forever.

Children of divorce need to trust in someone or something.

It becomes the single most important thread in the midst of all the pain and change. Trust is important to us all, and if our trust is violated by a person, we become fearful of trusting anyone else. These children need to be sure that the persons in whom they trust are not going to fail them or use their trust against their best interests.

One reason why Laura had so much pain in her life is that she did not trust anyone. She found it difficult to share her pain and resolve it because she had no one with whom to share it. She believed that if people knew how and why she hurt, they would use it against her. What Laura lacked was a caring faith community around her. She could have benefited from a strong youth group experience. But she trusted only herself, and even that trust was shaky.

Clergy understand the dynamics of trust. Pastors deal every day with people who are working through their problems by trusting their minister to listen to them. People place their trust in the clergy as they do in their very close friends. If these people ever fail them or violate their trust, the relationship is ended.

The pain that these children feel is tremendous. They have been hurt by their parents and are left to deal with things on their own. No one may ever have asked them to share their pain. If parents have not taken the time to listen to their children, why should anyone else? Too many children feel this way. Their trust level is diminished, and they do not want to invest the emotion in trusting someone else. It may take a long time to get a child like this to the point of opening up and sharing her or his pain.

Laura was able to keep hers buried for ten years. Talking to her was like going back to an unmarked grave and digging up the remains of past dreams and crushed hopes. She always tested the ground before she would commit herself to sharing her pain. She found it difficult to have a trusting relationship with friends, especially boys. She felt as if everyone would discover her secret pain and exploit it. She went from one bad relationship to another and never felt secure with herself.

If one parent fails in trust, it does not mean that the other one should follow suit. Trust in parents is the last thing a child should lose. Parents who lie to their children and break promises are destroying the trust level in their children. They need to know that their parents care enough to ask them how they are and help them work through the difficult times.

Friends, clergy, and teachers are the natural targets for children of divorce who may want to talk. These individuals may have the most to give these children as well. Some children may seek them out and test their level of commitment and trust before talking about their lives. It may take a long time before the children actually open up and share their feelings, but it is worth the wait. If they choose to talk about the pain the divorce caused them, it is up to us to listen to them and care for them.

Open or Closed Signs

It is difficult to determine when children are ready to start dealing with a divorce. One might hope that they would start dealing constructively with it during the actual proceedings; that is, it is preferable for parents to be aware enough to begin helping their children understand the divorce while it is going on. This will benefit the children further down the road. The parents have the advantage of taking their children step by step through this most difficult time of their lives. The parent who remains open during the divorce process will help his or her child to be open and sharing with feelings and fears.

Too often parents display the closed sign on their door and do not let the children in on the divorce. Being shut out means that the children are not important or that the parents are not coping with the situation themselves. This is difficult for parents to realize while they are going through a traumatic struggle of their own. Children will read signs differently from one parent to the other. Some children choose to put up their own closed sign and keep it there during the divorce. The parent who says that her or his children will not talk about the divorce is getting a closed sign from the children. The children may have gotten their closed sign from a parent or grandparent. At a time when the child really needs to talk about the divorce, someone shuts him or her out.

Some children keep their closed sign up all the time. Some are afraid to take the sign down and let anyone in. They are afraid to share their pain with anyone. If they keep the closed sign up, they reason, no one can hurt them again. They can stay in their own world and not have to deal with the hurt in their lives. It sounds good, but it does not always work. Sadly, some children have kept the closed sign up too long and have never dealt with their parents' divorce. Keeping closed has only caused these children more pain and resentment over the years. They have been left to deal with the divorce on their own, by choice and by our own closed signs.

Parents need to encourage their children to share their emotions and help them search through those feelings. Clergy and friends are in a unique position to be open to children of divorce. These children are looking for objects of trust, people whom they can share with, who are not going to hurt them, but will cry with them. They are seeking open signs to help them heal the pain of their broken lives. Being open means being interested in them and willing to take the time to care. The pastor or youth director who stops in just to chat is showing open signs that are encouraging to see.

I often wonder whether things would have been different if our pastor had been open to sharing with us about our parents' divorce. The old saying "Kids bounce back" does not apply here. Children can bounce back only if we adults are open to listening to them and their troubles. The children who do not find an open sign from a parent, teacher, preacher, or friend are going to keep their own closed signs up.

How to Risk Your Heart

Chip and Tracy were both very bright and energetic high school students. Looking at them, you would think they were brother and sister; in fact, they were. The only difference you could find in them was that after the youth meeting had concluded, Chip would go home to his house and Tracy to hers. Chip lived with his father and stepmother, and Tracy was just the opposite. If that was not enough for the two of them to handle, the future held more. The pain and changes from their parents' divorce was about to be compounded by not one, but both parents deciding to divorce again. The limit of trust and forgiveness was being stretched for both Chip and Tracy. Both their hearts were filled with incredible pain and fear. Who could they turn to for help and healing? With their homes in shambles, would their pastor be there to help them through this nightmare?

If we assume that children of divorce can find open signs in other people, then, and only then, can they risk opening their hearts to others. The most difficult challenge for children of divorce is the risk of revealing themselves to others. Sharing the pain of their parents' divorce is necessary but risky.

Some children are afraid to share their feelings with their parents. These children are fearful of hurting their parents by being totally honest with them. Some children simply do not know how to say what they are feeling. Parents who are open with their children need to ask questions about their children's feelings. Parents need to realize that they may hear things that might well hurt them. But they must remember that they are dealing with confused and hurting children who need to be encouraged to be honest with their feelings and not to feel foolish about asking stupid questions.

Risking the heart to a friend or pastor is a very real threat. If children want to share their feelings, they need to be assured that their thoughts and concerns are going to be kept confidential by a trusting person. These children really need the opportunity to vent their feelings in a caring atmosphere with people who will be understanding. This outlet will be a great opportunity for the children to deal constructively with their feelings concerning the divorce. If it comes early enough it can minimize problems later in life.

The longer children harbor their feelings about the divorce, the deeper they hurt. Children can carry the pain of divorce well into their adult lives. The past suffering can truly affect the way they develop relationships with others. By not dealing with the pain and hurt in their own hearts, they may not really know what a good relationship is. It becomes difficult to invest themselves for fear of the relationship's failure. For some it brings back too many memories of the past.

For Laura, any relationship was difficult. She was wary of people who really wanted to care about her or take an interest in her life. She constantly questioned people's loyalties and motives. She simply became fearful of trusting her heart to anyone. It took someone who had the interest and an understanding of her life to let her open up and share. Laura needed to know that it was all right for her to feel angry and hurt by her parents' divorce. She needed someone who was willing to let her cry out her pain and not hold it against her. She needed someone who was willing to care about her.

If a pastor, teacher, or youth director will take the time to ask the right questions, these children will respond. It may take a little time for them to develop trust and get over the fear of allowing someone else to see into their hearts. But once they give the open sign, they can be helped to recover from the divorce and move ahead in their lives.

Do not be shy about asking children of divorce how they are doing. Showing an interest in their feelings is a sign that you care. The pastor may not have all the answers or quick solutions, but does have the ability and the time to listen. They may not take the opening right away, but in time may come around. When they do, be prepared to listen and hear what they are saying. Let them tell their stories and share their pain.

VI.

Helping Children Cope with Divorce

People always feel compelled to offer understanding remarks to individuals who are suffering a crisis. To the weeping mother who has lost her only child, friends offer kind sentiments and understanding words, whether they have shared that same crisis or not. People show caring with great ease toward those who mourn the death of a loved one, but what comfort do they bring to those who mourn the loss of a marriage? How are individuals helped if they are a part of a struggling marriage? How are children helped to cope with the emotional strain that is placed on their lives?

Divorce is a grief process. The same feelings of pain, loneliness, and fear that accompany the death of a loved one are present in the divorce process. Children, especially, will mourn the loss of the marriage. For a young child, the separation from a parent as a result of divorce is similar to the death of that parent. The volatile emotions of the people around them only confirm their suspicions that something awful has happened in their home. Sudden, often rapid, changes in their life-style lead to further confusion and anxiety. Sometimes their only relief is to shut the whole thing out and deny that the worst has happened.

Children will close themselves up in their own worlds. They will imagine that the entire thing was a dream.

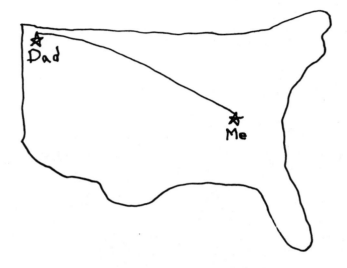

Tomorrow they will awaken and find their father and mother seated at the breakfast table, as if nothing at all had happened. Their fears will lead them from one fantasy to the next, until the reality of the situation finally sets in. The weight will crush them emotionally and leave them searching for a safe haven of rest. How will these children cope? Who will be there to help them sort through the jungle of emotions and doubt?

The minister who sits down with a child and talks about how he or she feels is actually helping that child cope with the divorce. The teacher who notices the pain in a child's eyes and cares enough to ask what's wrong is providing an avenue of coping to the child. We are all, in one way or another, capable of helping these children cope with the divorce. We falter when we do not know when or how to help. The when is always; the how is in each of us.

Some children will welcome the opportunity to talk about the divorce. The youth pastor might take a few minutes from the day to meet a young person after school for a sundae and some sharing. The pastor may want to stop by the child's home and spend a few moments just reassuring the child that the pastor is there when needed. Noticing the child's pain and letting the child know that someone cares is important.

Listening to Children

Few children are going to take the initiative to talk to the minister. We need to stay one step ahead of them and ask if they want to talk. They may not take the hint the first time around, but at least they know that someone cares about them. If concern for them is shown, eventually they will seek out that caring person and open up their hearts.

Listening to them can be as easy as any other conversation. They must be encouraged to share their story of the divorce, and you must listen with caring and openness. The child's reflection on the divorce may differ from that of the parents. Remember that each party comes at this situation through his or her own eyes and heart. If you are hearing about the divorce for the first time, do not try to read your thoughts into the situation. Let the child describe the divorce in the child's words and terms. Help the child to put feelings into words. By understanding divorce in terms of the grief process, we can better grasp the child's emotions and fears. All of us can relate to grief in various ways. If we listen to the story carefully we will hear the child's grief and pain.

Do not be too worried if your first encounter with the child is not a major success. It takes time to hear all the story and to sort through the rubble of the divorce. It may take a considerable amount of time to establish a trust level. The children may test the waters a bit before they open up. Trust is important for children. They need someone to share with, but they may wonder what people will think of them and how their confidences might be used against them. Trust shouldn't be confused with dependency. Trust is the basic assurance that what they share is kept between themselves and the listener. We who listen must assure them of our trust by being dependable and honest with them. The level of trust is very thin for children of divorce. They will test the people around them just to see if their word is true. If someone stands by them and passes all the tests, then they will share.

That seems like a lot of work—and it is. Listening should not be the only concern. The level of caring that the listener gives is the concern. Children of divorce will carry many fears with them through their lives. The fear of being disappointed once again is greater than others. When a young person comes to talk to a pastor, friend, or teacher, she or he seeks a listening ear and a reestablishment of trust. The listener has a great deal of responsibility. By listening and caring, you can help to raise the level of trust in these young people. Helping them cope with the divorce is first helping them understand the divorce. We help by listening to their story and looking carefully at their feelings and fears. The things that they share with the listener are avenues to their recovery.

Very often young people will go to a minister or friend because they do not want to talk to their parents about the divorce. This is not to say that parents cannot be good listeners. Parents can be great listeners if they can hear their children with an open heart and mind. Sometimes the children's view of the divorce is simply too difficult for the parents to hear. Too frequently parents do not give their children the opportunity to reflect on the divorce. Parents often think that if the children do not ask, things are fine with them. Some parents do not explore what their children are feeling. If parents are willing, they should ask; but they must be cautioned that it could be painful. A parent may hear unexpected things. Yet the outcome can be very beneficial to the parents and the children. They can resolve important issues face to face instead of allowing them to eat away at the children for a long period of time.

Touching Open Wounds

There is no doubt that divorce can cause serious pain to children, and that pain is ever-present and real on a daily basis. Children of divorce experience a grief situation with ghosts. The marriage may be dead between the parents, but it is not always dead for the children. The pain and frustration of the divorce linger around every day of their lives. Coping with ghosts is difficult.

Children of divorce struggle with the presence of two worlds: one where they live with the custodial parent, and the other where they have a chance to interact with their other parent. How to balance both of these worlds is troublesome for children. How do they cope with the reality of having two parents who are not together? How do we explain to them that this may be the best that it will ever be for them?

The trouble is in trying to understand the situation from their perspective. The minister or friend who listens to these children may find it difficult to relate to them. As the child relates the story, she or he will poke at wounds that are difficult to heal—difficult because it never seems to be finished. Divorce never stops hurting. Coping comes when we learn to live with the situation as it is. If we want to help these children, we must listen as carefully as we can. The caring listener will hear stories of hurt and frustration, guilt and anger. Sorting through these emotions will not be easy, but it must be done in order to help these children deal with their pain.

All of the pain cannot be dealt with at once. The listener must start slowly to build trust and gradually help the child piece together the different parts of the puzzle of his or her life. One hurt may lead to another. The victories seem so slight to these children. But by listening to them we can help piece together their own self-esteem and possibly clear away some of the misconceptions they have concerning the divorce.

The difficulty is that so much has happened to these children and so quickly that it is difficult to sort through it all. As we listen to them, we must continually keep the focus on their feelings and how they are dealing with them. We must help them verbalize their fears and frustrations. If younger children have trouble verbalizing, have them draw pictures of what they think has happened at home. Their drawings may reveal feelings of separation or fear. Older children are better at expressing their feelings and putting them into words. As we listen, we need to ask questions that will allow them to reveal more about their pain and hurt. The deeper they dig into the divorce, the more they can bring out into the open so it can be dealt with.

The more they reveal about themselves, the stronger the trust level grows between them and the listener. They will share their most important feelings with someone who is willing to listen and not make light of their situation. If they continue to share more of themselves, they are allowing an opportunity for true healing in their lives. Some of these children are afraid of the feelings they have about their parents and themselves. They want some way to make sense of all of the change and hurt. We can help them to cope by dealing with each fear and anxiety one at a time. None of this is going to be solved in a few hours of tears and talk. The pain of divorce runs deep within these children. They have had to grow up too fast and assume too much responsibility too soon.

Helping them to cope is giving them time to sort through the wounds in their lives. Remember, they may not be alone in this. A pastor, teacher, or youth advisor may need to listen to two siblings at the same time. Listening takes time—time to help them sort through their feelings about the divorce as well as their feelings about themselves. The greatest victory in dealing with children of divorce is helping them to recover themselves. They need to know that they are still important and are capable of being loved.

Leave the Door Open and the Light On

Learning to cope with the divorce does take time. It would be nice if these children could awaken to find that their parents' divorce was all a dream. The pain of the divorce is never over quickly. The time it will take to learn to cope with the frustration and pain may never really be enough. Some of the hurt and resentment will linger for a long time to come. Coping is difficult to achieve as long as the children are looking back at what they have lost. There are pieces of their lives that they will never recover. The memories will be of painful times in their lives rather than good. They will always be searching for ways to handle their emotions over the divorce.

The missing pieces of a child's early life can never be replaced. Too many children of divorce are forced to grow up faster and assume more responsibility than they should. This hurried tour through childhood leaves some children yearning to go back. You can never go back in a divorce. Too much has transpired to be able to turn back the clock. Caregivers and listeners need to continually challenge children of divorce to move on in their lives. Too often they choose to close the door on themselves and not move beyond the pain and frustration.

The self-esteem of many young people is shattered during the divorce. It is an easier course to simply hole up within themselves than to challenge the world around them. They need to be encouraged to risk a little of themselves, one step at a time, and reestablish their own lives. They have taken a major step by just seeking someone out with whom they can open up. The door must be left open for them to recover from the divorce and pass through, on to the rest of their lives. Too many young people are standing at the threshold of recovery and just need some indication that they can move beyond their fears and anxieties to new opportunities.

This is not just limited to young people and children. Many adults have never recovered from their parents' divorce. Much pain and frustration is being played out in everyday life by young adults who are still hurting from the past. Troubled relationships, difficulty in making deep commitments, and the fear of trusting themselves to others can all go back to their past divorce experience. These adults never learned to cope with their parents' divorce. No one ever asked them if they were hurting or paused long enough to listen. Now these young adults are starting their own families and bringing the past with them.

The sooner a child or a young person can find the opportunity to share his or her divorce story the better. Whether it is with a pastor, teacher, parent, or youth leader, these young people need to talk. Will they find persons to listen to them? Will the church be aware of the crisis in the pews today? How often will a pastor pass by a young child in tears and never ask how he or she can help? If the moment is left to slip away, then all the child will remember is that the door was closed and the lights were off.

VII.

The Divorce Is Never Over

This should have been the happiest day of Chris's life. He was about to be married to a charming woman whom he had met in college. But on this day, all that Chris had hoped for was not to be. He had wanted this day to be perfect in every way. He wanted most of all for his parents to be there and share in the joy of his marriage.

Months earlier, he talked to both of his parents and invited them to the wedding. At first, his mother seemed thrilled at the thought of her son's marriage. Later, after she learned that his father would be present, she tried to find some excuse not to attend. Chris's father was the same way and refused to attend if his mother was present. Chris was married that afternoon, without either parent present.

Chris's parents were divorced five years before he got married. Five years of not having a real family life. Five years of bitter arguments between his parents after they were divorced. The divorce of his parents was a continual problem to Chris. They spoiled his high school and college graduations by not attending them at all. At every turn in his life they were there to bring up the ugly past of the divorce. They never considered how their actions might affect Chris. They only considered how their lives affected each other.

Children of divorce never escape the divorce of their

Dad

Mom

parents. The trauma and pain will stay with them for the rest of their lives. They may learn to cope with the pain and deal with the separation, but they will never be through with the divorce. At the most important times in their lives, when one would expect parents to be present, these children may have to make do with only half or none.

Whether the children are young or old, the effects that divorcing parents can have on their children is far reaching. Just when children think the pain is over and life can continue again, they hit a rut in the road. The young child who wants his dad present at the school Thanksgiving pageant suddenly realizes that his dad is truly gone from his life. Do we give any thought to the young girl who is left out of the mother/daughter banquet at church, because her mother is not there anymore? All the seemingly normal functions in life are often not available for children of divorce.

If we look, it can be seen every day of our lives. At school, at home, and even in the church, children of divorce are going through life with half of what they had. Most church programs today are designed for the family, without consideration for the children of divorce or their single parents. When was the last time a parent/child banquet was held in a local congregation?

Children of divorce go through life with the baggage of their parents' divorce firmly in tow. This was not their choice, but our society has not begun to recognize the extreme hardship these children are under. For them the divorce will never be over, because there are too many pieces missing from the puzzle of their lives. Their real regret is that others do not understand why they still hurt after all these years. Why are there still ghosts in the closet of these young lives? Why, when they reach out, is not someone there to care about them?

It Still Hurts Today

Years beyond their parents' divorce, young people are still trying to deal with their pain and resentment. The issues of the divorce may be different, but the struggle is still the same. At high school graduations and weddings, young people are still being hurt by their parents' divorce. The long-term effects on children of divorce are just now being studied.

How the divorce of their parents affects the lives of these children today is an important issue for the local church. These young people are the present members of many congregations across the country. They will bring with them the lingering effects of their parents' divorce. They will come to the church, looking for someone to care about them. Some will come for healing and comfort. Do not think that this is news. Children of divorced parents have been in the local church for years, but few have been recognized in the pew.

Children of divorce are no different from other children. They have the same hopes, dreams, and aspirations as the other children around the church. These children are already participating in most church functions and giving a great deal. What they lack in life is a caring community around them. They need help in dealing with past and present pain in their young lives. Most need restoration of their self-esteem. The local church is one place where young people from divorced families should be able to find a supportive, loving community. They need the fellowship of other young people and the professional concern of the clergy. They are still hurting, after all these years, because few have cared for them. The church is one place where they may turn for caring.

The challenge is to see that these children are able to continue to deal constructively with the divorce. Pain and resentment may still be evident, years after the actual divorce. Some young people are still struggling with a tremendous amount of guilt and anger over their parents' divorce. Learning to build healthy, trusting relationships with others can be difficult for children of divorce. Some cannot seem to find any sense of hope or renewal in their lives. They have kept so much within themselves that it may be too much of a struggle to just let it all go and risk their hearts once again. Children of divorce have a tremendous fear of failing in relationships and also of being rejected by others. So many children of divorce possess a terribly low self-esteem. They find it difficult to engage in relationships and reveal their true selves. The hurt is still there from the divorce experience, and even the passing of time cannot heal all the wounds.

These young people will be a part of the congregation at some time. They may be in a youth group or church school class. Some will be members of a divorcing family in the church. Others will come from other towns with their hearts already burdened with the pain of their parents' divorce. The local church will have an important role to play in their recovery. Hopefully, the church can be ready to receive them and help them heal. The church will need to be accepting of these young people. Some children will need to share their burden with a pastor or youth director who is willing to listen to them. Others will need the simple assurance that they are loved and important. The local church will not become their shelter, but rather a place of quiet rest and healing.

It Takes Time to Heal

The old adage that time heals all wounds may be true. The healing process for children of divorce will take some time, but it must be time well spent. For children of divorce, time can be seen as an asset or a liability. Too much time that is spent dwelling on the pain and resentment can be destructive for these children. Conversely, time that is well spent and directed toward healing is positive. Children do not bounce back from divorce overnight. It may take years for them to get a handle on their emotions and set their world in order.

One reason for having the parents follow their children through the divorce, facing the problem now and not later, is to be able to cut through some of the time lag between divorce and recovery. Parents who are open with their children throughout the divorce are better able to help them prepare for the future. Sharing with the children along the way can clear up some of the misconceptions and doubts the children might have. Children are better off dealing with the conflicts of divorce in the present rather than later in their lives.

The process of healing emotional wounds is never easy. The more help the children can get early on, the better they will cope with the divorce. This means that at the very onset of the divorce, parents and clergy need to be aware of the children's needs. The alarming fact is that too few persons take the time to help these children soon enough in the healing process. Too much time can pass before a parent or pastor realizes that the children might be suffering from the divorce. Not until they see the anger or sense the resentment do some parents finally catch on. By then too much time may have passed.

Too often parents miss the signs their children are giving. Some children start to get very depressed during the divorce. They become closed and move off to be by themselves. School work sometimes begins to suffer, and they lose interest in outside activities. Some children become very possessive of the custodial parent. Nightmares may begin to occur on a regular basis. These are signs that it may be time to talk with the children about their fears and doubts.

This is the place where the church and the clergy may be most helpful to the children. The pastor who is dealing with a family in divorce can help give the parents positive directions in which to move. The pastor may be able to suggest a local support group for children of divorce and one for the parents as well; many local churches now sponsor such support groups. The pastor or youth director may also counsel the children and help them sort through the divorce process. These are positive steps in the right direction. The more constructive time the children can have in dealing with the divorce, the better off they may be.

Some Do Bounce Back

In time, most children do begin to cope with their parents' divorce. If they are given time to sort through their parents' divorce, and if there are caring individuals around them, children of divorce can live a very full and rewarding life. The reason that so many children struggle with the divorce lies in their not having had the opportunity to grow beyond the pain. Many children have recovered from their parents' divorce because they have taken the risk of opening themselves to other people. Caring clergy, friends, and parents have offered these children the chance to deal with their pain and hurt.

First, these children must be recognized as the innocent victims in their parents' divorce. After we begin to understand their pain and confusion, we can start to give them the help and comfort that they deserve. The healing process is important for children of divorce, but few have taken the opportunity to provide a means of healing for them. The pastor may take time to talk with both spouses throughout the entire divorce, and even afterward. But how much time does the pastor spend with the children? Divorces occur every day in our society. Parents are hurt, grandparents are hurt, and so are the children. Each participant in the divorce is desiring of the care and attention a pastor can give, but, in the long run, it seems that the children are coming in last. Their future may very well depend on how they are cared for during the divorce. They cannot be expected to simply grow out of their parents' divorce. The damaging effects of divorce will not fade with age, but may grow deeper into the lives of these children. The children who wrestle with their own pain and fears can win themselves back, if there are people around them who care.

It will take time for children to bounce back from the divorce. During their time of healing, clergy, parents, and other caregivers need to help them realize how important they are to themselves. It will take time to build their self-esteem back up again. The wounds of the divorce will be hard to heal if they are left open too long. These children will need to know the grace of forgiveness and be taught the joy of reconciliation. Bouncing back can mean putting an end to the past pains of the divorce and helping them look into the future of their lives.

The young people who have been mentioned earlier have all bounced back from their parents' divorce. They were able to achieve this success because of caring individuals in their lives. In many cases it was the parents who helped, but for the most part it came through caring clergy and friends. These people took the time and, in some cases, made the sacrifice to help these children of divorce see a better tomorrow. Not all young people have success stories. Some children need a great deal more time and caring before they can begin coping with their parents' divorce and start toward a better day.

Caring clergy, parents, and friends have made a difference in the lives of children of divorce. If we can understand their situation and help them through the divorce, their lives will be better because of our caring and concern.

VIII.

Stepfamilies

Eric was ten years old when his parents divorced. It was difficult for Eric to adjust to his parents' divorce. He still struggled with anger and resentment over the divorce. Somehow his life was just not the same without his father and mother together. The divorce settlement named Eric's mother as the custodial parent, with visitation rights for his father every other weekend. During the next two years, Eric grew accustomed to the fact that his parents were never going to get together again. He was fortunate enough to be able to stay in his same home and school. The visits with his father were nice, but they never replaced the real experience of having his dad around the house.

After the divorce, his mother took a job as a secretary downtown. It was at work that his mother met another man, and she started seeing him on a regular basis. The whole experience of his mother dating was strange for Eric. Phil was a nice guy, but Eric still struggled with the notion of a new man in his mother's life. Eric was not sure what was going to happen to himself. If his mother married Phil, who would Eric live with? He loved his father very much and hated the thought of having a stepfather. Eric began to worry about all kinds of questions concerning his life. The thought of a stepfather worried him the most. He felt that if his mother got

married, he would have to stop seeing his real father altogether. He wondered whether this new man in his mother's life would be as nice to him after the wedding as he was now.

Eric's questions and worries are no different from those of millions of other young people in his situation. Nearly seven million young people live in stepfamilies today. The Step-Family Association of America estimates that almost one-third of the children born in the United States during the 1980s will live with a stepparent before reaching eighteen years of age. In 1980 almost 6.1 million children lived in stepfamilies. In 1985, 6.8 million children lived in stepfamilies. Stepfamilies account for a large percentage of American families today. The new American family is the stepfamily.

One thing to keep in mind is that most stepfamilies are born out of failed marriages. The pain and struggle of the divorce is often carried over to the next marriage. Coming out of the pain of a divorce and into the confusion of a stepfamily can make for a very rocky road ahead for any set of parents and their children. Even if the stepfamily is fostered out of the death of one of the parents, there can still be difficulties down the road.

When we think of stepfamilies today, we cannot see them in the same light as they are depicted on television or in the movies. Being a stepfamily does not mean that every day will end happily or that solutions are easy to find. Real stepfamilies have a different set of problems that are unique unto themselves. You cannot blend two separate families together and then not expect some difficulties and challenges. Issues of parenting, communication, and loyalty are important in a nondivorced family structure, but these issues are crucial to stepfamilies. Stepfamilies are instant families that need special planning and care if they are to succeed. According to the Step-Family Association of America, 50 percent of marriages begun since the mid-1970s are likely to end in divorce. For second marriages, the estimated divorce rate is 60 percent. As many as one-third of the children born in the 1980s may live with a stepparent by the age of eighteen.

To be a stepparent today is a very real challenge. It takes time, planning, and a great deal of communication with everyone involved. The children of stepfamilies have an equally difficult challenge before them. Children of divorce must face the realization of having several different parents. Questions of loyalty, love, and resentment are important issues for these children. The ghosts of the divorce still haunt them, even in adulthood. One expectation of the stepfamily is that the new family will heal the old wounds. This is not always true. There may be a new "mother" or "father," but that does not always mean a new parent for the children.

Many struggles and questions will be raised along the way. The pastor or caregiver who deals with the parents or the children can help in many ways to avoid extreme difficulties for the new family. Parents must be made aware of some of the problems they will face along the way. How do parents help their children prepare for a remarriage? Do children resent their parents for dating someone else? How do we teach families to communicate openly? These are important questions to be raised when we talk about stepfamilies. We must realize that stepfamilies are a part of our everyday lives. They shop in our stores, live in our neighborhoods, and worship in our churches. But not all of them are the happy families we might perceive them to be.

Dating and Children

Shortly after my mother separated from my father, she started dating. She never really told us that she was going to start seeing another man. I guess it had started out as a casual date with some of my mother's friends, but it became serious during the following year. On the occasions that we had to be with him, he always brought his two children along. It all seemed innocent enough, until my mother's best friend informed my brother and me that this was to be our new father. It was then that I knew I did not like him. I had a father, and one was all I thought I needed. If my mother wanted to have a new husband, that was her business, not mine. My mother married shortly after the divorce was final. She seemed happy enough with her new husband, but it changed my life forever.

It is an odd feeling to have one of your parents start dating. Both of my parents went through the process of dating and remarriage. Handling the courtships of our parents was difficult at times for us kids. It is hard for a child to imagine his or her parents seeing someone else, let alone marrying someone else. Children have a strong sense of loyalty when it comes to their parents. Being separated from one parent through divorce is difficult enough for children. When you add to that separation a new stepmother or stepfather, you begin to complicate the feelings of insecurity and fear with which the children are already trying to deal.

Parents who are trying hard to take care of their children during the divorce process must also be careful if they choose to remarry. Most stepfamily conflicts occur because of a lack of adequate communication with the children. It may be important for a single mother or father to remarry, but she or he must prepare the children for this remarriage. It can come down to the question of, "Do I marry for myself or for the children?" Parents need to take their children into account during the decision-making process. They need to share with their children their desire to date or to remarry. If this news comes out of the blue the children will start out on the defensive. Parents must be willing to discuss their own feelings with their children, and the children should have the opportunity to share their own fears or questions over the possibility of becoming part of a stepfamily. The couple who show up in the pastor's study to talk about their remarriage should already know where the children stand in the relationship. The pastor must ask the couple whether they have considered the children's feelings about their marriage.

Taking the children into consideration should start from the beginning, usually with the first date. Planned activities with both families or the prospective spouse are very helpful. Parents can see how the children might interact in the new relationship. Parents should not be discouraged if things do not go well at first; it takes time to warm up to a new person and other children. This is a new area for any child to adjust to. Care must be given to see that the children are not forced to fit into the plans too soon. One planned activity is not going to tell all about the future of the marriage. The children may be resistant to the changes that are posed by the marriage. Parents need to take the time to ask the children about their feelings. The children may need to be reassured that their love for the noncustodial parent is still important. They need to know that they are not expected to give up or replace a father or mother because the custodial parent wishes to remarry.

Ministers might even suggest that the wedding ceremony include the children from both families. This type of involvement allows the children to feel as if they are a part of the decisions and future of the stepfamily. Having a son stand up with his father or a daughter as a maid of honor to her mother can go a long way in establishing a healthy foundation for the new family.

Communicate Openly

One of the most important elements of any new stepfamily is communication. Talking about discipline, getting to know the other children, and learning likes and dislikes come through verbal communication within the family. If only one lesson has been learned from the failure of other stepfamilies, it is the role of communication. More stepfamilies are being started every day of the week in the United States than first marriages. The key to helping these stepfamilies to survive is to teach them how to communicate. The role of the clergy is paramount with this issue of communication in the new family. The church is able to play an important role when it joins these families together. The church will either help them prepare for the challenge of being a stepfamily or it will stand by and watch them fail. Clergy have a great opportunity to help these new families to succeed.

With the blending of two families or the adding of a new spouse to a fragmented family comes some amount of conflict and resistance. If parents have taken the time to introduce the possibility of a stepfamily early on, the conflicts might not be too difficult. It is possible that the children have had enough time to adjust to the new situation and have moved toward some sort of acceptance. This does not mean that there will not be some difficulty in adjusting to new people or a new home. It does mean that the parents are making a move in the right direction.

Communication must be open from the beginning. The newly married couple must especially take time to avoid their own conflicts by sharing their feelings. Stepfamilies will take a longer adjustment period. Balancing the children, a new home, and a new relationship can take a great deal of work and effort. The children must know that they are free to share their own feelings within the relationship. Without the freedom to question and be a part of decisions, the children might become angry and resentful of the new family structure.

The new stepfamily can be difficult for children in many respects. For one, it raises the pain of the divorce all over again. The children might resist the new family structure because it really does not replace the one they believe was lost through the divorce. Feelings of loyalty start to surface toward the parent who is missing. The new stepparent is not like the parent the children know still exists. The whole grief process starts to unfold within the stepfamily. These feelings need to be shared in a healthy, open atmosphere. The children must be assured that their natural parents are still an important part of their lives. Visitation privileges should be maintained, and the lines of communication must stay open with the ex-spouse for the benefit of the children.

It is a good idea to establish a family sharing time during the week. The parents must make sure that the children understand that they can share their concerns openly. Questions of discipline, household responsibilities, and school can be a part of this discussion period. The stepfamily must be able to openly discuss all their concerns. Children should not be afraid to talk about missing a father or mother. Holidays should be planned so the children can spend some time with both the custodial and the noncustodial parent. The children's taking a vacation with the noncustodial parent can provide a great break for the new couple and a rewarding visit for the children.

When communication is open within the stepfamily, most issues can be confronted and avoided before it is too late. The balance is difficult and very demanding, but the rewards can be great. Children will survive the divorce and the stepfamily if there is enough thought and caring from the parents. Every day stepfamilies are struggling to keep it together and wondering where they failed. They falter when they do not talk about their problems and fears. They fall apart and lose their children's love when the couple ignore the new family to pursue their own goals. The home the children thought they had was destroyed once; it should not happen again.

Time and Patience

Having an instant family does not mean that problems do not exist. Millions of men and women are stepparents today. They have learned that it takes time and patience to become a successful stepfamily. Time that is spent sharing with the new spouse is equally as important as time shared getting to know the new children.

Too many stepparents try to hurry through the process of becoming a stepfamily. They want to marry one day and unpack the next and expect everything to be fine. When things do not work out within the family, they believe the marriage is the cause and eventually divorce again. Not enough time and patience were given to the marriage or the family. Couples that do not communicate within their relationship usually are not talking with their children either.

The new couple must work hard at their relationship from the very beginning. Parents in stepfamilies have more work to do than in a normal first marriage. The honeymoon period may be only a short drive from the church to the house. Now they have a family that is grown and ready to put the new couple to the test. They may have been parents to their own children, but now they must learn new faces and names and personalities. The adjustment period for these new parents is very short, but the new couple's relationship cannot be sacrificed from the start. Parents need to take some time to chart their new course and decide where they are going to start. The demands of the stepfamily will draw a great deal on the emotions of the parents.

Parents should not expect too much too soon. If

stepparents expect a happy home overnight, they will be disappointed quickly. It takes time and patience to raise a family, even a stepfamily. Sharing with the children together is an important part of the process. Parents should not set their expectation levels too high. A success one day may mean defeat the next. Taking one day at a time is enough. More and more parents are finding help with stepfamilies through support groups in their neighborhoods. Many local churches are starting and sponsoring support groups on a weekly basis. Sharing with other parents in the same situation can be nurturing, and support groups are a wonderful opportunity to see how other parents handle similar problems within the family. These types of support groups are not limited to parents only. Children are learning to deal with the adjustments of being a stepchild in similar support groups all across the country.

Even though stepfamilies can have their share of problems, they can be a wonderful experience. For some children, a stepfamily may be the only real taste of what a true family is. With work, patience, and a willingness to share, most stepfamilies can succeed, and clergy need to take the time to prepare the parents for some of the pitfalls of stepfamilies before and after the ceremony. Divorced individuals who are planning to remarry are in church pews every week. Thus the church must be prepared to minister to the parents and their children.

Much of the clergy's work will come in pre-marriage counseling sessions. Ministers need to share with these divorced parents some of the opportunities and hazards of the stepfamily. Clergy are concerned with making sure that persons are prepared for marriage. Most parents should welcome the opportunity to plan ahead for the up-coming marriage. Pastors should ask how much the children have been involved in the couple's dating. Have the two parents taken the time to share with the children what their plans are for the immediate future? Has the couple discussed the addition of new children to the marriage? If a never-married person plans to marry someone who has children, is that person prepared for the role of instant parent?

The same thought should be given to second marriages. How many pastors have asked an individual or a couple if they have grown and learned from the first marriage? Too often couples go into a second marriage without having dealt with the pain of the first marriage. The pain and anger of a failed marriage should not be carried over into the next. This can be very destructive to the new couple's relationship and may impair the health of the stepfamily.

Clergy and caregivers must also be mindful of the children in stepfamilies. This is a tough adjustment period for a child. The children may struggle against the addition of a stepparent. Yet these people are still parental images and cannot be dismissed as "Mom's new husband." Clergy can help them see the opportunities and benefits of a new family. Too often the children tend to dwell on the negative aspects of the stepfamily and never really give it a chance. The children can be encouraged to share their feelings with their parents and be open to the changes that a stepfamily brings. Parents must be careful not to make too many changes too soon. The children need time to adjust to a new environment, and so do the parents. The children need to have some say in the decisions that are being made. What should the children call the new spouse? What are the expectations of the new stepparent for the children?

Parents must also establish a united front in the areas of authority and discipline. Too often the children will play the two parents against each other in order to get their own way. The most important thing to do is to give the stepfamily time to develop. Stepfamilies should not be forced into a mold. These families are unique in almost every aspect. With time and patience, the new stepfamily can grow into a wonderful, healthy family.

IX.

Divorce in the Church

Allen and Carol are in their late thirties and have two teenaged children. The family have been members of St. Matthew's Church for several years. In fact, Carol grew up as a member of St. Matthew's with her parents, who are still attending the church. A little over nine months ago Carol stopped in to see Pastor Turner. Carol's session with Pastor Turner was very difficult. She shared her pain concerning her marriage to Allen. Carol did not believe that the marriage could continue much longer. A few months earlier, she discovered that he was having an affair with a woman in his office. When Carol had confronted Allen with the affair, he at first denied it, but later admitted that it was true. Despite all of Carol's efforts, Allen decided to leave her and the children for the other woman. That was when Carol decided to seek some advice from Pastor Turner.

Carol was having a terrible time handling the break-up of her marriage. Her parents were upset and angry with Allen, and the children were becoming difficult to handle at home. Carol needed help from her pastor. She did not know what to do next or how to handle all the emotion of the situation. Divorce, for her, was a terrible thing and against her own beliefs. Now she was faced with a broken marriage, angry parents, and two children who were terribly confused.

Pastor Turner tried her best to comfort Carol in the face of this difficult situation. She suggested that they try to work out their difficulties and possibly seek some professional marriage counseling. Over the course of the next few weeks, Pastor Turner tried to get Allen and Carol to sit down together and see if they could salvage their seventeen-year marriage. None of Pastor Turner's efforts seemed to help, however. After several weeks of visits and talking, the answer was clear. Allen filed for divorce from Carol. The children and Carol were able to stay in the house, and Allen was going to take an apartment in town. Carol continued to see Pastor Turner on a weekly basis. Together, they tried to put some order back into the chaos of Carol's life, but not once did Pastor Turner offer to talk with the children. She understood that her role as pastor was to be a helper and guide to the members of her church. But are not the children a part of her congregation as well?

Scenarios like this have been repeated in the local church

more than one would like to admit. The church is not immune from the trauma of divorce. If anything, the church is probably the place where the effects of divorce are the most telling. There was a time when divorce in the church was seldom heard of, or so it seemed. Most individuals involved in divorce would leave the congregation and not return. It was a scandal to have a divorce in the church thirty years ago. Most couples could not take the scrutiny and the questioning of the congregation; they quietly slipped away from the church. The church also struggled with the difficulty that divorce presented. The divorce of a couple was against the teachings of the church and therefore put the church in a bad light. Even though the church understood the dynamics of divorce, it struggled with how to be of help to divorcing couples. Even now the church is still searching for ways to heal the wounds of divorce.

Seldom in the past did the church do anything to help divorcing couples. Except for pastoral counseling and some professional marriage support groups, the church has had little to say or do for individuals and children of divorce. Through the years the church has struggled over the demise of the American family structure. Unfortunately, the church has had little impact on this area of concern. The church's emphasis must be on encouraging better family life from beginning to end. The enrichment of marriage is a vital tool in recapturing the core family structure. We no longer deal with the odd divorce here and there. The church must place an emphasis on helping couples establish a strong family structure from the beginning of the marriage. Marriage enrichment and family development seminars may help foster a better family in the future, but today is a different story.

The church today is faced with more divorces than we have ever known. Week after week, marriages are failing at an alarming rate. Today the life expectancy of some marriages may be as short as three years. Many of these marriages involve young children. In the church today there are more divorced, single parents than ever before. These parents are a part of the congregation today because they choose to be. The role of the church is to reach out to them, try to help them recover from their divorces, and restore their children's hope. How can the church help restore these individuals and meet their needs? How does a congregation minister to the needs of children whose lives have been shattered through divorce? The church must be there to help heal their lives and show them the grace of God.

An Open and Caring Congregation

When news of Carol and Allen's impending divorce reached the congregation the reactions were varied. Some members were sympathetic to Carol's problem because of Allen's infidelity. Still others thought the two of them should be able to work things out. For the most part, the members were shocked and saddened by what had happened. Allen and Carol were involved in many aspects of the congregation's life. Carol sang in the choir and taught a church school class, while Allen was the chair of the finance committee and a part of the men's fellowship. For a time, neither of them attended worship services. Each was afraid that the other might be in church that morning, and did not know how to handle the situation. Carol chose to drop out of the choir for a while, and Allen resigned as chair of the finance committee because of time conflicts. Everyone knew that the two were struggling with their divorce, but the members of the congregation did not know what to do to help them.

Divorce is a difficult experience in a congregation. The pain of separation that the couple feel is compounded by the constant questions and whispered rumors around the church. Most individuals do not know what to say or how to help during a divorce. Whether the couple is family or just good friends, we find ourselves at a loss as to how we can comfort and care for them. We know that these people are hurting, but how do we help them through this experience?

One of the constant issues that confronts church members when there is a divorce in the congregation is that of taking sides. If the couple have family members in the church, the issue tends to be complicated. If another member is a good friend of the couple, who does that person turn to first? If a few men are supportive of Allen during the divorce, does it mean that they approve of his actions? Carol's family has been a part of St. Matthew's for years. The congregation has watched Carol grow up in the church and feel a real affection for her, but now they are unsure of how to help or whether they should be involved at all. It may be easier to talk about it in the women's group than to do anything at all. Pastor Turner was constantly being pressured for little details of the divorce. She advised only the well-meaning members to pray for the couple and their children. Prayer can be a great comfort, but it does not replace a positive, healing approach to the situation.

Congregations every day are being faced with the failure of marriages. Most congregations weather these storms in quiet resignation, waiting until the clouds of rumor pass, and then going on about their business. A local congregation should be a place of healing and comfort. We preach and teach the practice of love and reconciliation, but find it difficult to cope with broken relationships in our own sanctuaries.

The role the local congregation can play in divorce is substantial. Couples and children going through divorce need the comfort and understanding that a congregation can offer. If there is a death in the church, the congregation is more than willing to help and comfort a grieving family. Divorcing families are grieving in the church today. The church is not a place to take sides in a divorce. Congregations should be even in their caring for both the individuals and their children. Whether the theology of a particular church believes that divorce is a sin, the church is still in the practice of teaching forgiveness and reconciliation. It is hard to be even in our caring. Some would rather not take sides and simply leave the situation to resolve itself, but it should not be like that in the church.

Faith communities need to be open and caring toward individuals who struggle with the problems of everyday life. If the church practices its caring toward individuals who are struggling through divorce, it may well help them to recover from this difficult experience. Through a congregation's love and concern for divorcing couples, the lessons of forgiveness and healing are brought to the forefront of everyday living. By not taking sides or shunning one individual, we learn to be a caring faith community. Congregations need to understand that when people are dealing with the difficulties of life, our caring is most needed.

Some denominations have turned to using a liturgy of divorce. In the presence of a worshiping body, the marriage is dissolved and the individuals are still affirmed as members of the body of Christ. This does not mean that a church must have a special service in order to continue to support and love divorcing couples. It could simply be that congregations need to draw attention to forgiveness first, not dwell on past sins. The ministry of reconciliation might take on a new meaning, if faith communities were to embrace these couples and help them to heal from their pain.

The preacher in the pulpit should echo the forgiving grace of God as the congregation embraces the difficult issue of divorce. The ministry of the church is a ministry of all believers. The clergy may have to spend considerable time working with divorcing couples and their children. This is time that is well spent and very beneficial. The congregation has a role in this ministry also. The congregation may not wish to support the decision for the divorce, but it must be willing to support the hurting individuals involved in the situation. It is proper to pray for these people, but it is also important to embrace them and find ways to help them through these difficult times. The church's help could be as simple as developing a support group for parents and children of divorce. A congregation could offer to help with child care while a young mother works or assist in finding the financial resources to help pay for marriage counseling. Even after the divorce the congregation must be open to the changes that may occur. One spouse may leave after the divorce, but it must not be seen as the fault of the other spouse. Some divorced members will remarry. The addition of a new face, and possibly new children, will prove to be an opportunity for the congregation to embrace a stepfamily with love and caring.

The church can show its support for the family. The issues of parenting and building stronger marriages are just as important as support for divorced individuals. There is still a strong, healthy family structure in our society. The church should be offering support classes and workshops to its families on a regular basis. If the current families are encouraged and equipped, they may not fall into the dilemma faced by divorced families.

A caring and open faith community can mean a world of difference to a couple in divorce. The children, in particular, can benefit from the nurture and love of a congregation that is open to helping wherever possible. These individuals are members of the parish and need the compassion that can come only through a community of faith. Down the road the children of divorce and their parents will remember the role the church played in their lives. The difference the church makes now may be the difference these people make in the church later.

Keeping in Touch with the Children

One of the more essential roles the pastor may play is in helping the children of divorce. These young people are some of the most neglected individuals in the entire divorce

105

process. Too often these children are left entirely on their own to deal with the pain of the divorce. If the parents are not helping them through the divorce, who is? Clergy, youth advisors, or other caring individuals in the congregation have a real opportunity to minister to these children's needs.

Clergy have the opportunity to interact in their members' lives on a variety of levels. Many know the members of their congregation on a personal basis. Thus most clergy will be involved some way during the course of the divorce. The pastor may spend a considerable amount of time with the parents as they work through their problems.

It is hoped that the pastor is in touch with the young people of his or her congregation. If the pastor has spent time getting to know the church school children and the young people of the youth group, he or she should have no trouble establishing a level of trust with a child involved in divorce. Spending specific time with a child of divorcing parents is really showing these children that the pastor does care. The child may see the pastor as an independent person with whom she or he can share. The parents should certainly welcome the opportunity to have someone they trust and respect helping their children understand the divorce.

The pastor or youth director who shares with young persons must be very committed to sharing with them. No one should ever try to convince a child to see things in favor of one particular parent. The role of pastor, friend, or youth advisor is be objective and honest. The listener is there to help the child understand his or her feelings and to see the divorce in its true light. Whether it is a child working through a divorce or a young person who is now a part of a stepfamily, the child deserves the benefit of caring and loving clergy.

The pastor needs to start as soon as possible to listen to these children. If too much time passes before the pastor shows any interest, the opportunity may be lost. The child may find another person to share with, or simply close up and not give anyone the opportunity to help. It may be as simple as asking the child out for an ice-cream sundae after school or stopping by the youth room on Sunday evening just to ask how they are doing. The pastor should not limit help to just one of the children, but should try to counsel all of the children in the family. It may be appropriate to talk to the children one on one or in a group setting. How the pastor chooses to meet with the children is not as important as how soon she or he takes the opportunity to do so.

In some instances it may not be the pastor who has direct contact with the children. It may be a youth director, teacher, or close family friend. All of these individuals are capable of serving as significant others for the children. Caution needs to be given so that the children do not become dependent on the pastor or teacher. The listener is not there to replace the role of the parent. Anyone who takes the time to care for these children is a welcomed friend. The listener needs to be reassuring of the children, but always moving the children forward in their recovery.

Keeping in touch should not be limited to just the children of divorce. Children in stepfamily situations will need the same sort of caring and listening. These are children of divorce also, but they have added the dynamics of working through a new family setting. These children will start to relive their own divorce experience in the stepfamily. They will struggle with questions of loyalty and resentment and will worry as their mother or father begins a new marriage. This is a difficult adjustment period for the children. As the pastor works with a couple's wedding plans, he or she needs also to be thinking about the children who are involved in this second marriage. The pastor needs to ask the children how they are adjusting to a new person in their lives. Are there problems that the pastor needs to share with the couple before the wedding? The children may need to see that a stepfamily can have some positive results in their lives. One thing children need is a positive, stable environment.

A stepfamily may give the children a new start in their lives, if they are open to the situation.

If the pastor, youth director, or church school teacher is open to sharing with these children, they can build a wonderful relationship. Caring individuals can have a positive effect on children of divorce. The opportunity is there to teach them how to build a healthy relationship based on trust. When helping children to heal the wounds of divorce, the caregiver can teach children the value of forgiveness. More important, they can learn that they are important individuals and that there is hope for the future. If anything, these children need to know that the world has not come to an end.

Practical Congregational Ministry

A few months after Carol and Allen's divorce was final, Pastor Turner received a visit from Allen. She had a feeling she knew what the visit with Allen was going to be about. Allen's request was simple: He wished to be remarried at St. Matthew's. On the surface, Allen's request seemed ordinary enough, but it would put Pastor Turner in a very difficult position.

Allen was still a member of St. Matthew's. He had been attending the early worship service, because Carol was singing in the choir during the later service. When word of Allen's remarriage reached the congregation, Pastor Turner's phone started to ring. Carol was the first to call to see if the news was really true. Carol thought it odd that Allen would want to be married in the same sanctuary where they had taken their vows. She had hoped that this situation would not come about. Carol understood Pastor Turner's position. What could she do in a situation like this? Allen had every right to request to be married at St. Matthew's. He was still a member of the church and was entitled to the sacrament of marriage. It was difficult because the congregation did not know how to handle the situation. If Allen had gone somewhere else to be married, there would have been no problem. Carol's parents were disturbed that Pastor Turner would even think of performing the ceremony of a man who had hurt their daughter so much. The more the congregation talked, the worse the situation grew.

Throughout the next few weeks, Pastor Turner wrestled with the question of Allen's remarriage. Would the situation have been different if it were Carol who was getting remarried? Chances are the congregation would not have been as concerned as they were about Allen's marriage. Most congregations are merely large families anyway. They feel for some of the other members the same way that they feel about their own relatives. Too often congregations see one individual as the victim and the other as the villain. Pastor Turner knew that she had to treat this situation carefully, and soon.

The following week, Pastor Turner made it a point to talk to each of the persons involved. She shared with Allen and his fiancée her willingness to perform the ceremony. She suggested, though, that they be married in the chapel and not in the main sanctuary. She cautioned them that it might be best to keep the ceremony simple and small. From the beginning Carol had understood the position in which Pastor Turner found herself. She wanted to make it clear to Carol that this was not a personal issue in her mind. As the pastor, she had the authority to perform the wedding ceremony for Allen. Had it been Carol that was remarrying, Pastor Turner would have acted in the same manner.

Pastor Turner's last visit that week was with the vestry committee of St. Matthew's. She knew that many of the members of the committee were concerned about the pending wedding. She believed that now was the time to see if the words she preached on Sunday morning were worth the paper they were printed on. There was one thing that she wanted to make clear about her decision to perform Allen's wedding. In her view, she did not feel the church was in a position to be selective about who should be forgiven and for what. Certainly, Allen had made a serious mistake that harmed many people. But is the church not the place where forgiveness and reconciliation should begin? Here was an opportunity to show the same patience and forgiveness that Christ had shown for the thief on the cross. Her contention was that St. Matthew's was, first, a congregation of practicing believers. Second, she believed that the church had an opportunity to minister to Allen and Carol as they worked to forgive each other and move on in their separate lives. The work of the church is the healing and reconciliation of broken lives. The needs of Allen and Carol's children should also be a concern of St. Matthew's. Whether it is in death, divorce, or baptism, the church has before it the ministry of forgiveness and reconciliation.

Pastor Turner faced the same difficult decision that many clergy are confronted with today. How do pastors truly minister to couples and children in divorce? It may be easy to let these situations resolve themselves. Pastors can remove themselves from confronting these difficulties by refusing to perform the weddings of divorced individuals. All that does is alienate a few more people from the church. The pastor is safe, and the couple has gone down the street to City Hall. Many denominations have started using services of divorce as a part of their liturgy, but the church still struggles with the issue of remarriage. There is a place for ministry in the local church with divorced people and their children. If the church is willing, it can be the greatest blessing to those who hurt and are searching for some peace in their lives.

The difficulties of divorce will never be far from the sanctuary door. Clergy will see the effects of divorce in the pew, the classroom, and the fellowship hall of every church in our country. Clergy will look out over their confirmation classes and see many children with just one parent present. From the marriage service to the graveside committal, divorces will touch the church. The grandparents, who may not have seen their grandchildren since the divorce, will share their pain in many a pastor's study. In the church and in their homes, the members of our churches will know the saddening effects of divorce.

Support, Support, Support

In the church today the need is evident for caring and concerned clergy to help these people find peace. Practical parish ministry may not be practical in their case. The ministry that these individuals need must be a bold step in a new direction. In some ways it may mean a departure from our old traditions and a move toward a more challenging understanding of the gospel. If the church is not prepared to minister effectively to these people, they may go elsewhere, possibly away from the church altogether.

The parents and children of divorce need a church setting that is open to ministering to their needs. Churches need to understand how they can be supportive of all persons involved in divorce. The church and our society have hardly begun to understand the far-reaching ramifications that divorce has on the children. Generations of young people are growing up in our communities without a healthy understanding of marriage and a family. They are moving through the churches of our country, searching for support and direction. From parent to child to grandparent there is need for a caring, supportive community to help heal their pain.

It will not be difficult to organize and direct a support group for divorced individuals, children of divorce, or stepfamilies. It does take time and commitment on the part of the church. Church boards will be happy because support groups do not cost much. Any church that has an open classroom is capable of hosting a support group for these individuals. Many churches already have invited Alcoholic's Anonymous and Weight Watchers to meet in their churches.

111

Why not have divorce support groups as a part of the guest list?

Congregations must first decide that they are willing to organize a church-related support group for these individuals. Some congregations are reluctant to open their buildings to just any community group. This should be a ministry of the church that invites the community to participate, not the other way around. Once the board or session has given the go ahead, the stage is set to begin.

The pastor should be involved from the beginning to give direction and to keep the organization on the right track. The pastor does not necessarily need to be the single person in charge, but someone must be in charge to call the group together and plan the sessions. There may well be a divorced individual in the congregation who has had a successful recovery from his or her divorce and who might be willing to convene the group. One option is to ask a local family counselor or psychologist to preside. Whoever that convener is, he or she must be dependable, able to take control of a sizable group, and firmly committed to the ministry of the support group.

The convener must pick one evening for the support group to meet and maintain that schedule. It takes a deep commitment to this type of ministry. If the meeting session is moved from one evening to the next, with no pattern, it will get lost in the shuffle of other scheduled activities. People appreciate knowing that when they show up for a meeting, it will actually meet on the evening that it is scheduled.

Sessions should not be more than two hours in length. People are usually tired from the day's activities and may not be able to keep their attention span focused for more than two hours. Smaller groups are much easier to work with. A group of ten to fifteen individuals is a comfortable size. If the group grows beyond twenty it might be advantageous to form another support group. The sessions should be open enough to share important information and plans for the next session, but the convener should not let the session wander. It is important to have some structure, but do not allow the session to become so structured that there is no freedom to explore those issues important to the participants. Remember that this is a support group and not a singles' club. Socializing is important, but the issues are support and growth.

The format of the sessions should be open and positive. Participants may want to begin with a prayer or a simple devotion. It is important to remember that these sessions are a way to help build support among the participants. At all times, the sessions should be treated as confidential sharing. Hearing statements that were meant for the support group repeated outside the session can harm the trust level that should be developing. Participants should be encouraged to share their divorce experiences and how they are dealing with the situation. Focus should be kept on sharing helpful advice and not just on telling the same story evening after evening.

The convener may wish to have special speakers come and share with the group. Good resources found in any community may be a local psychologist, family counselor, or pastor. Guest speakers should be asked to deal with specific issues and concerns. Make sure that there is adequate time for questions following these presentations.

Many support groups have benefited from adopting particular study books from which to draw program topics. There are many good books available today that concentrate on divorce recovery. There are also a few videotape series for divorce support groups. A local family counselor can be a good resource for subject material.

As a support group grows, so will its influence and trust. More people will come if they hear that the group is positive and refreshing. Support groups should be capable of celebrating with persons who find healing and peace within themselves. The faces will change from time to time as persons grow in their lives and move on in their relationships. Others will leave because they have found the ability to have a new relationship and choose to marry again. Those are the rewards of being in a support group. These groups are not an end in themselves, but a means of building up persons who have suffered and need healing.

Many individuals can benefit from a support group. Stepfamilies and children of divorce are finding a great deal of comfort and strength through support networks in their communities. These types of groups can be organized along the same lines as a support group for divorced parents. Some support groups for parents and children meet on the same evening, with the children in one session and the parents in the other. It can be a great benefit to stepfamilies to share experiences and advice together. It reminds them that they are not alone. Children sharing with other children can also be a positive experience. When the children have an opportunity to face the divorce with the support of other children facing the same experience, it can aid in their healing and recovery.

Support groups for children of divorce should be held in a small-group setting of no more than ten children. Too many young people will make the group difficult to work with. The convener should be someone who can relate easily with children and be able to keep their attention on the issues at hand. It is best to have a group of this nature meet for a short period of time. The focus and content of the sessions should always center on dealing with the children's feelings and difficulties concerning their parents' divorce. The convener should always be supportive and positive with the children.

Outside speakers, such as a child psychologist, can be a great resource for children's support groups. There are also many good books available for children to use. The convener may wish to augment the sessions with special topics or a video series.

The methods for structuring a support group for stepfamilies are similar to the first two mentioned. It is possible for a support group to be designed for stepparents only. This gives other stepparents the opportunity to exchange information and ideas without the children present. At the same time, a separate group for the stepchildren could be meeting down the hall. There may be times that the group sessions could be combined to enable the whole stepfamily to address specific issues and concerns.

The rewards of support groups can be great. The healing and the comfort brought forth from these sessions can spell the difference in the recovery and healing of parents and children. The congregation will notice that some of these people will be in the pews come Sunday morning. Because the local church has reached out to them and cared, they may wish to be a part of that type of loving community.

The role the church can play with children of divorce, divorcing parents, and stepfamilies is very important. The clergy, teachers, or friends who take the time to share with the children of divorce are doing a great work in the world today. Even though divorce is so prevalent today, it might be changing in the future. If the church will consider seriously its role with children of divorce and help in their healing, we might start to raise a different generation of husbands and wives. These children know the pain of divorce and do not want the same thing to happen with their children. The marriages of these children will be stronger and more experienced. They will try harder when they are faced with difficulties in their marriages. They may well build a new foundation for the family structure, but they must be cared for now, while they are still a part of the church and can be reached. If they are left to drift away, they may never be recovered.

If my pastor had stopped to talk to me that summer afternoon when my dad left, maybe my life would have been different today. How many other young lives could be different today if a pastor, teacher, or friend had cared

115

enough to ask a child how he or she was dealing with the parents' divorce? Too many children of divorce have already slipped through the parish door, without having had the chance to recover from their parents' divorce. Each day, some ministers will counsel with the parents about their divorce and not think of the children left at home. Millions of children are waiting for the opportunity to talk with a pastor who cares enough to ask them if they are hurting.

Support Group Guidelines
for
Children of Divorced Parents

— Gain permission of the church board for the establishment of a support group for children of divorced parents.

— Select a convener or group leader. This can be the pastor, a trained professional, or an individual who has recovered from his or her parents' divorce.

— Choose an evening that is relatively free for most members of the group. Once you have established the meeting night, stay with the same evening on a regular basis.

— Keep the group size to ten-fifteen individuals. Too large a group will not allow enough quality interaction.

— Structure the meeting time for about two hours. This gives time for socializing before or after. A forty-five-minute presentation by an individual will allow for a period of questions afterward. Announcements of future events can be made either before or after the session.

— Be careful to plan social activities on an evening other than the regular meeting night. A visitor would feel uncomfortable walking in on a party.

— Presenters and speakers are readily available in most communities. Books and video series are also good sources for programming.

— Alternating between speakers and group sharing time can be very effective.

— It can be beneficial to share some of the responsibility with others in the group. Select a program coordinator, refreshment host, and a person to share a short devotional.

— The convener must keep the evening on track. You do not want the group to wander from its purpose.

— Always keep the focus on recovery and moving ahead.